REEL LIVES

Michael Doherty

RTÉ

Published in association with
Radio Teilifís Éireann

BLACKWATER PRESS

© Michael Doherty

First published in 1995
by Blackwater Press,
Unit 7/8, Broomhill Business Park,
Tallaght,
Dublin 24

Printed at the press of the publishers.

Editor: Anna O'Donovan
Design: Philip Ryan

ISBN: 0 86121 617 2

CONTENTS

TAKE ONE

When Blackwater Press approached me with a view to writing a film book, I always had it in mind that the finished project would reflect the style and approach of my *MovieGuide* column in the *RTE Guide*. As a result *Reel Lives* blends interviews, features and quirky film facts, with a quiz section which will test the mettle of most movie fans.

The interviews contained here have previously been published in edited form in the *RTE Guide*. For the purposes of this book, I have reverted to the original tapes to provide the full transcription of those face-to-face encounters.

With this in mind, I would like to thank Heather Parsons, *RTE Guide* editor, for her permission to use the interviews; and to other colleagues at the Guide – Mick, Donal, Teresa, Edwin and John C – for their help along the way. Thanks, too, go to Michael Croke at CEL and to John, Anna and Philip at Blackwater Press. A special vote of thanks to all the interviewees included in this book, and to the film companies – UIP, Buena Vista, Columbia Tristar – who supplied most of the photographs.

Finally, I thank my family for their love and support. This book is dedicated to them. And to F.

"If we bring a little joy into your humdrum life, it makes us feel as though our hard work ain't been in vain, for nuthin'."

Lena Lamont "Singin' in the Rain" *(1952)*

REEL 1

NATURAL BORN DIRECTOR

Quite simply the hottest property in Hollywood, 28–year–old Quentin Tarantino's first feature, Reservoir Dogs, became the benchmark for cinema chic and introduced audiences to a distinctive blend of violence, humour, and the snappiest dialogue this side of Raymond Chandler. Earlier scripts such as Natural Born Killers and True Romance were snapped up by A–list directors Oliver Stone and Tony Scott, while hip actors queued up to take part in Tarantino projects. When we met, his second film, Pulp Fiction, had just scooped the Palme D'Or at the Cannes Film Festival and would go on to win the Best Screenplay Oscar and take over $100 million at the US box–office.

Seated in his hotel room in London and dressed in a plain black suit and black tie (straight out of Reservoir Dogs*), the former video–store clerk is famously hyper, enthusiastic and a man who eats, drinks and sleeps movies...*

Michael Doherty

First of all, can I say that Pulp Fiction *blew me away, in every sense of the word...*

Quentin Tarantino

Thank you very much. Supercool! Good to know it went down well in Ireland. You know I was over in Ireland myself, a couple of months ago. I went to Connemara and drove around. It was wonderful, I just loved it.

__MD__ *Any chance of shooting a movie there?*

__QT__ No, but I might buy a house there sometime! It was incredible.

__MD__ *Working on* Pulp Fiction, *as opposed to* Reservoir Dogs, *meant a bigger budget, bigger stars and the involvement of a major studio. Did that cramp your style?*

__QT__ No, I'd have to say it didn't cramp my style. With *Reservoir Dogs*, we had like a million point three to make a movie and we tried to make it look like an eight-million dollar movie. Here, we had eight-million-dollars and we tried to make it look like a twenty-million-dollar movie. Having that bit extra solved a lot of problems. Now I hear that Harvey Weinstein is showing the movie to Disney executives in America to prove that such a thing can be done!

__MD__ *Eight million dollars would be less than Bruce Willis's normal pay cheque. How did you entice him aboard?*

QT He was totally into the movie; he just wanted to do the part. Most of the actors took pay cuts of some kind, the most drastic being Bruce's. But we didn't think, "Oh, we'll just pay them this little salary because they want to do it." We picked them all up at a good price, plus points, and, at the end of the day, everybody is going to end up doing very well out of *Pulp Fiction*.

MD *Was this ever going to be three separate films or was* Pulp Fiction *always in your mind from the outset as a montage of three stories that intertwined?*

QT These three stories, yes. They could have each been expanded to become their own movies but the stories were always designed to come together as *Pulp Fiction*.

MD *The masterstroke of casting in this movie has to be the return of John Travolta as Vincent Vega. Did you have him in mind from the outset?*

QT Oddly enough, I wrote it for another actor [Michael Madsen] and, about one third of the way into the movie, I met John and discussed the fact that I wanted to work with him at some point. We got together and had a really good time and everything. I left thinking, wow, this could really be an interesting way to go. Then the actor I wrote the part for opted out to make another movie before I had finished writing it, and John stepped in. It is hard to imagine anyone else as that character now.

MD *Was that twist sequence between John and Uma a nod to Travolta's Tony Manero in* Saturday Night Fever*?*

QT It was actually there when I wrote it for the other guy but it adds an extra edge for John. He's in this café where there are all these icons – Marilyn Monroe, James Dean, Buddy Holly – and you don't think about him much when he is sitting there with Uma Thurman. But when he gets up on the dance floor, it's like, it's not just Vincent, he's an icon, too! He's not a wannabee, he's the real thing. It was never designed that way but was one of the benefits of having John in the film.

MD   *In the opening shot of that particular scene, the camera follows John Travolta as he enters the diner and tracks him around the room. It is a shot redolent of DeNiro arriving in to the bar in* Mean Streets *or Ray Liotta walking into that club in* GoodFellas. *Was it a deliberate Scorsese homage?*

QT   I wasn't actually trying to do a *Mean Streets* on it. The whole thing about that place was, I had built this gorgeous diner, Jack Rabbit Slims, from the ground up, for the movie. And the thing is, whenever you have a really great set, you just want to show it off! I had a long scene to do so I thought, OK, what I'm going to do is follow John in, and through him I'm going to show the audience the whole crazy contraption of a place. Following him around is just a way of getting you into this weird, other world.

MD   *The diner in question is filled with cult film posters, particularly Roger Corman titles,* Machine Gun Kelly, Sororiety Girl, *etc. What's the story?*

QT   Well, the whole idea was that they would be Fifties, delinquent-type movies and they were all hand-picked by me. Out of the eight posters, four or five of them are Roger Corman films because I've always been a huge fan.

MD   *How important was the Palme D'Or to you? Has it made you more bankable, are more people answering your calls? Or is it just the icing on the cake?*

QT   Well, it's not so much that I'm more bankable but it's about the most prestigious award you can win as a film-maker, even more so than the Oscar. It's great to win and I think that it will mean a lot to the film in Europe and in America, too, where it hasn't gone down so well until now. For me, though, it's the show of recognition for this kind of film-making that's important. I take my movies very seriously and I take the Palme D'Or very seriously. But, at the same time, I don't take myself very seriously.

MD *Was there added pressure on you to come up trumps with* Pulp Fiction *since* Reservoir Dogs *had been such a critical success? In other words, were there people out there just waiting for you to fall?*

QT Well, I didn't really pay much attention to any of that. Journalists were saying to me after *Dogs*, "Do you feel the sophomore jinx will hit you?" I never thought about that. I was really happy with the script I had written and the film I was making. My feeling is, if you're happy with the movie, it's all the same whether they throw roses or tomatoes at you at the screening. It's nice to get roses but at the end of the day, it's how you feel about the movie that counts.

MD *What stands out in your films is the snappy dialogue and slick verbal exchanges which I suspect are the main reasons so many actors want to work with you. Are you somebody who sits on the subway listening out for phrases?*

QT When I hear a snappy turn of phrase I try to remember it. But usually when I am writing, the characters just start talking to one another, so the dialogue is kind of being created at the time.

MD *How important is Harvey Keitel to the career of Quentin Tarantino?*

QT Very important. He set me on the road by helping to get *Reservoir Dogs* off the ground. He supported me personally because he is sort of like my father. He is a very important person to me and I love him very much. As an actor, he is one of my favourites and I really enjoy using him.

MD *The natural extension of Keitel is to use DeNiro. Any plans?*

QT Well, I just recently met DeNiro and we really hit it off. There are a lot of actors I am anxious to work with but I really want it to be right. I want the marriage between them and the role to be perfect.

MD *The timing would seem perfect for a DeNiro/Keitel collaboration. When they started in* Mean Streets, *Keitel was the lead but it was DeNiro's career which really took off. Now, following* The Piano, Bad Lieutenant *and* Reservoir Dogs, *Harvey himself is right up there.*

QT Exactly, and what I would really like to do is put Harvey and DeNiro together again now that Harvey's fortunes have changed. Right now it is at a perfect epiphany for those two guys.

MD *I know you don't like to talk too much about* Natural Born Killers, *but the film was advertised in the States with the tagline, "'A little Tarantino goes a long way". How do you feel about that?*

QT I haven't seen the film and it isn't really what I wrote any more: it's Oliver Stone's thing. It is doing well in America and I wish it well, but I don't really feel I had anything to do with it.

MD *Are you an easy man to work with and work for?*

QT I think I'm real easy to work with! Everybody who has ever worked with me wants to go on working with me. Miramax and I get on like a house on fire. I want what I want but I can hear more than the sound of my own voice. It's not like I'm always shouting, "Just do it!"

MD *As a passionate film fan who worked in a video store surrounded by other people's films, do you still feel like a kid with a toy when you get your hands on that camera and then see your name in lights? Or has it lost some of its lustre?*

QT No, it's not as incredible as it was before because this is what I do now. It's my life and it's what I want to do for the rest of my life. But the lustre hasn't gone away at all. And it's very important to keep that bit of amateur in you. I was at the Venice Film Festival recently, walking around really taken with it all, when it struck me: gosh, what other business could I be in where I could be here, having travelled the world with my film? Wow, what a business!

POSTSCRIPT

As we finished our interview, Tarantino noticed my Warner Brothers notebook, containing photos of Cagney, Flynn and Bogart on the cover. Exclaiming "Supercool!", he picked it up and drew the following picture of his interviewer (who had been introduced to him as a writer for "Ireland's version of Time Out *magazine").*

MOVIEGUIDE'S 10 FAVOURITE FEMMES FATALES

1   "You're not too smart; I like that in a man." Kathleen Turner, *Body Heat* (1984).

2   "OK, Mister Ed. Let's have a look." Linda Fiorentino (below), *The Last Seduction* (1993).

3   "There's a speedlimit in this state, Mr Neff." Barbara Stanwyck, *Double Indemnity* (1944).

4 "Sometimes the truth is wicked." Gene Tierney, *Leave Her To Heaven* (1945).

5 "Why don't you go outside and jerk yourself a soda?" Annette Bening, *Bugsy* (1991).

6 "It took more than one man to change my name to Shanghai Lily." Marlene Dietrich, *Shanghai Express* (1932).

7 "I think it's good business to surround yourself with ugly women and beautiful men." Rita Hayworth, *Gilda* (1946).

8 "You are scum. I'll be right over." Laura San Giacomo, *sex, lies and videotape* (1989).

9 "You're a painter, paint these!" Joan Bennett, *Scarlet Street* (1945).

10 "Sometimes I know exactly what you are going to say. The other times; the other times, you're just a stinker." Lauren Bacall, *To Have and Have Not* (1944).

TAKE
TEN
RODDY DOYLE

The section in which various personalities have been given three minutes to answer ten revealing questions about their cinema-going habits. First up is Booker Prize–winning author and screen-writer, Roddy Doyle, whose novels The Commitments *and* The Snapper *have both been made into successful films by Alan Parker and Stephen Frears, respectively.* The Van *is currently under production.*

1   *If you were to be stranded on a*   *Amarcord* (Fellini; 1960, It.), *The Quiet*
     desert island with nothing but a   *Man* (Ford; 1952, US) and *Reservoir*
     VCR and three films, what titles   *Dogs* (Tarantino; 1992, US)
     would you choose?

2   *What was the most recent film*   *The Northerners,* and I'd rate it seven
     you saw and how would you rate   out of ten.
     it out of ten?

3   *When was the last time you cried*   It was at the John Sayles film,
     at the movies?   *Passion Fish.*

4   *Who was your first movie star pin–up?*

Believe it or not, I never had one. I never pinned up a movie star in my life.

5   *Who is the actor or actress who most makes you want to throw your popcorn at the screen in disgust?*

Rick Moranis, I think, although that wouldn't be strictly true because I never go to see anything with him in it! But there are one or two others, like Shirley MacLaine. So, Rick Moranis and Shirley MacLaine.

6   *What is your attitude to sub–titles?*

I'd much rather sub-titles every time. I hate dubbing.

7   *Who is the finest actor or actress you have ever seen?*

Alison Steadman (*Abigail's Party, Life Is Sweet*)

8   *Can you name the Magnificent Seven?*

I'll try. The difficult one was Horst Bucholtz, wasn't it? Yul Brynner, James Coburn, Steve McQueen. That's four. The Man From Uncle, Robert Vaughn, was it? That's five, but I'm lost with the other two.

9   *If Hollywood were planning to film the story of your life, who would you like to see in the title role?*

Lemme think . . . John Goodman!

10   *And what would it be called?*

The Short–Sighted Ex–School Teacher.

BROKEN DREAM

Marilyn Monroe

'Goddess' n. 1. a female deity. 2. a woman who is adored, esp. for her beauty (Oxford English Dictionary)

Hollywood over the years has produced its fair share of stars and starlets, heroes and heroines; but talk about a film goddess, and you can mean only one person, Marilyn Monroe. For the short time that she was in the public eye, Monroe single-handedly personified the glamour and seduction of the silver screen. She occupied more column inches, more unauthorised biographies and more bedroom wall space than any other actor, before or since.

"Every man's love affair with America" is how Norman Mailer described her, and the glorification and peddling of that image took precedence over any contribution she made to the silver screen. Marilyn Monroe made close on 30 films in her 12-year career, yet if you put a gun to the head of the average person in the street, they would be hard pressed to name half a dozen. It was never about Norma Jeane the actress, it was always Marilyn the icon that obsessed the world.

"God gave her everything," said Billy Wilder, who directed her in the films that everyone does remember, *The Seven Year Itch* and *Some Like It Hot*. "The first day a photographer took a picture of her she was a genius." That day in question occurred in 1945 when an 18-year-old aspiring model and actress, Norma Jeane Mortenson, was snapped by Army photographer David Conover, who felt that the young lady had

certain "inspirational" qualities. Within a short space of time, Norma Jeane had been voted "Miss Flame-thrower" by one unit and "The Girl Most Likely to Thaw Alaska", by another. Meanwhile, the Seventh Division Medical Corps elected her "The Girl We Would Most Like to Examine".

For the young girl from LA who had grown up without a father, whose mother spent lengthy periods in asylums and whose childhood consisted of being shuttled from foster home to foster home, it was the first taste of adulation: an adulation which she craved but which was fickle in the extreme and would eventually desert her when she needed it most.

At the age of 25, on the strength of a few brief but telling movie appearances, Norma Jeane became Marilyn Monroe (Monroe was her mother's maiden name, Marilyn Miller was her favourite musical star) and signed a seven-year contract with Fox Studios worth $500 per week.

Even at this early stage, the press had less interest in her future plans as an actress than in her recent appearance as a nude pin-up.

Marilyn didn't deny that she had been paid $50 by photographer Tom Kelley for the famous calendar shot ("Sure I posed nude," the actress commented. "I was hungry") but it was a more provocative exchange that set the agenda for future relations between La Monroe and her public. "Didn't you have anything on?" asked one reporter. "Sure," answered Marilyn," I had the radio on."

Marilyn Monroe was quickly filed under "blonde, bimbo, bombshell," and the label was reflected in the quality of the films she was offered. The more Marilyn wanted to promote the actress, the more Hollywood was interested in the goddess. "Big breasts, big ass, big deal," moaned the star. "Can't I be anything else?"

The simple answer was no; she would not be allowed to become anything else. Hollywood had a perceived image of Marilyn and, while the actress had good reason to feel aggrieved at how she was treated, she was not entirely blameless. Rather than discourage the press's insatiable appetite for titillation, Marilyn went along. "Do you wear falsies?" they enquired.

"Those who know me better, know better," she replied. Her celebrated penchant for dispensing with underwear had a similar effect on a voyeuristic public.

The delineation between Norma Jeane the actress and Marilyn the goddess came to a head in 1954. That year, Marilyn starred in *The Seven Year Itch* and proceeded to make cinema history by standing on a subway grating in front of the Trans Lux Theatre, her white skirt billowing about her. While Billy Wilder was filming the scene, 20,000 New Yorkers stood by, ogling as take after take revealed more and more of those famous legs. Meanwhile, 14 electricians were at each other's throats in an effort to be the one standing below the grating operating the fan.

Amongst the throng that day was Joe DiMaggio, Marilyn's second husband (she had married James Dougherty as a 16-year-old in 1942, they divorced four years later), who was far from enamoured. The marriage between Marilyn and the Yankee Clipper survived only a few more weeks, lasting eight months in all. DiMaggio remained loyal to

Norma Jeane (sending flowers twice weekly to her tomb at Westwood), but had little time for the Marilyn circus.

After *The Seven Year Itch*, and tired of her perceived image, Norma Jeane left Hollywood and enrolled at Lee Strasberg's famed Actors Studio in New York. She took her drama classes very seriously and produced the performance of her career in her next movie, *Bus Stop*. "As near genius as any actress I have ever seen" was how director Joshua Logan summed it up. Despite the acclaim, Marilyn found it increasingly difficult to be taken seriously. While she surrounded herself with weighty tomes from luminaries such as Rilke, Whitman, Milton and future husband Arthur Miller, the public chose to believe that few of these books were well thumbed.

Wedding number three, to playwright Miller, took place in 1956 and the press had a field day. "Egghead Marries Hourglass" screamed the headlines, shattering once again any illusion Marilyn might have had of becoming intellectual by association. After she expressed an interest in playing a heroine from Dostoevsky, for example, Billy Wilder tersely commented that he would be happy to direct Marilyn not only in *The Brothers Karamazov*, but in a series of sequels beginning with *The Brothers Karamazov Meet Abbott and Costello*.

One man who understood the difference between the on-screen and off-screen Marilyn persona was Laurence Olivier, who had a harrowing time directing and appearing opposite her in *The Prince and the Showgirl*. Despite various problems on the set, which almost drove the most celebrated actor of his generation to distraction, Olivier recognised the Marilyn magic: "For certain rare people, whose gifts are almost invisible to the naked eye, a miracle takes place in the tiny space between the lens and the negative. After working a very short time with Marilyn Monroe, I learned to trust this miracle and stopped gnawing my fingers by the side of the camera."

"Hollywood is a place where they'll pay you $50,000 for a kiss and 50 cents for your soul," said Marilyn, and no one was more qualified to comment. Even now, the public ignores her contribution to the cinema and remains obsessed with the rumoured miscarriages, the abortions, the drug abuse and the dangerous liaisons with the Kennedy clan. Her untimely death at the age of 36 is surrounded by more than a whiff of scandal and continues to be a favoured topic of conspiracy theorists.

At the end of the day, it doesn't matter if Marilyn died after swallowing 47 Nembutal tablets (accidentally or otherwise) or if she was murdered by anyone connected to the Kennedys, the CIA, the FBI or the Mafia: it was the Hollywood beast — the all-consuming, unrelenting parasite which was instrumental in creating Marilyn Monroe and responsible for destroying Norma Jeane Mortenson — which killed the beauty.

REEL 2

LEAN, MOODY AND MAGNIFICENT

Born in London in 1958, the son of Poet Laureate Cecil Day–Lewis and actress Jill Balcon, Daniel Day–Lewis toyed with the idea of becoming a cabinet–maker before the acting bug struck and he enrolled at the Bristol Old Vic drama school. Since making his blink–and–you'll–miss–him screen debut in Sunday Bloody Sunday *(1971), his film appearances have been relatively selective, but the roles he has chosen have left him in no danger of becoming typecast: a gay cockney in* My Beautiful Laundrette *(1985), an Edwardian fop in* A Room with a View *(1985), a native American in* The Last of the Mohicans *(1992), and an Oscar–winning Christy Brown in* My Left Foot *(1989), to name but a few. A bout of* Hamlet–*inspired nervous exhaustion led him to keep a low post–Oscar profile but that didn't prevent his name being linked with a group of women who*

are complete strangers to the ugly stick – Isabelle Adjani, Winona Ryder, Julia Roberts and Juliette Binoche.

Returning to the screen with a vengeance in 1994, Day–Lewis took the lead in Martin Scorsese's The Age of Innocence *and Jim Sheridan's* In the Name of the Father. *Seated in a hotel room in London, where he has arrived to promote* The Age of Innocence, *the 35-year-old actor looks entirely at ease. Tall, rangy and clad entirely in black, Day-Lewis is every inch the head–turner, and it was a fascinating experience, when walking through the hotel with the actor after the interview, to watch the reaction of the women in the foyer as the penny dropped...*

Michael Doherty:

Between finishing Last of the Mohicans *and starting* The Age of Innocence, *there was a gap of only five months. Was that enough time to make the switch from an eighteenth-century Indian to a nineteenth-century socialite and get a handle on the new character?*

Daniel Day-Lewis:

It seemed like longer but probably about three of those months were spent in rehabilitation because we were all fairly broken down after filming in North Carolina. We had bits hanging off us! But I had already spoken to Marty before I worked on *Mohicans* and we had decided to go ahead with *The Age of Innocence,* and that's something I very rarely do regarding future work. I seldom know more than one film at a time in advance. I had been thinking about Edith Wharton but it wasn't a case of getting a handle on the character. I don't really know what that means.

MD: *In the sense that, for Anthony Hopkins, finding a moustache in props gave him the handle he*

needed to play Mr Wilcox in
Howards End.

DD-L: The moustache, yes. Maybe I
do need something like that
but it's not something I look
for and I'm not very aware
of finding a key so that
other things will fall into
place. My way of working,
which is quite indecipherable
anyhow, seems to be a much
muddier kind of thing. I
flounder apart in a quagmire,
looking for nuggets which
may or may not be there.

MD: *I suppose if there is one thing,*
physiognomy apart, that is most
often said about you, is it that
you are a perfectionist who will
go to any lengths to achieve
total immersion in a role. In
The Age of Innocence *you*
worked with Scorsese who has
been most associated with
DeNiro, the method king. Was it
a meeting of kindred spirits?

DD-L: Well, Martin wasn't the first
perfectionist I have worked
with but he is a unique kind
of perfectionist and I am
always enthralled by people
who can worry over what, to
others, might appear to be

insignificant details in the
way that Martin does. I feel
very drawn towards that. I
appreciate the fact that there
is somebody who shares the
same kind of insanity and
recognises the rather
eccentric kind of freedom
that is needed.

MD: *While I was watching your*
portrayal of Newland Archer, I
was reminded of Montgomery
Clift in The Heiress *(1949). Was*
that an influence?

DD-L: Not a conscious influence
but it was certainly a film I
had seen and a film I
watched again shortly before
we worked on *The Age of*
Innocence. Montgomery Clift
as a performer has always
intrigued me.

MD: *Do you enjoy working on an*
intimate film like My Left Foot
or do you prefer running through
streams with tomahawk flying?

DD-L: Well, having had the rare
privilege to indulge in both
things, I am happy to say
that different yearnings have
been fulfilled! I suppose if I
were pinned down into
making a choice, which I try

not to do, I would say that I prefer a more intimate working situation. The scale of *The Age of Innocence* might seem grand but the central working situation was of an intimate kind. It is a conceit but basically you try to create for yourself the false impression of privacy within a public situation, because shooting is always very public. Sometimes that is hard to do because the machinery of the film is hugely distracting. But that's part of the battle.

MD: *You've always struck up a good rapport with Jim Sheridan. What is it about him that seems to bring out the best in you?*

DD-L: When you meet him, you will know almost immediately. I have rarely met anybody who has met him who hasn't wanted to strike up that kind of rapport!

MD: *What is it about Ireland that impels you to spend a lot of time there, rather than, say, doing the Hollywood circuit of power lunches?*

DD-L: My father, I'd say, first of all. My parents took us to Ireland as young children and encouraged us to think of the place as a home. We didn't need a lot of encouragement because we were enthralled by the place. My sister and I have retained that sense, while away, of longing for it, and while there, of pleasure about it. I very often feel that I don't make choices but that choices seem to make themselves. To live in Ireland doesn't seem like a choice; it appears to be right.

MD: *You were invited to go to Sarajevo for their Film Festival in the company of Vanessa Redgrave, among others. Why was it important for you to get there and why do you think the bureaucratic heads denied you the opportunity?*

DD-L: It was important, primarily, because we were invited and it seemed an important gesture to accept that invitation from people who were struggling to lead a fuller life. When you watch news reports from that area, they inevitably concentrate on the ducking of bullets and the level of starvation and these are, of course, the primary issues. It is a horrendous situation, people are living under siege and dying unnecessarily. But it is also true that people are trying to live their lives, as well. The universities and cultural activity continues. Susan Sontag, as you know, put on that production that caused all sorts of controversy outside Sarajevo, but the people there were happy that the lines were being kept open.

MD: *What direct help could you have provided?*

DD-L: Some people are able to give medical help. We are a group of film-makers and it is all we have to offer. If we are invited to offer that, it is something you feel you should do your best to go through with. We didn't take the decision lightly. We were to take our seats on the plane after the aid workers and after the press had taken theirs. We didn't feel, in that respect, that we were abusing the system but it became a bit of a fiasco, unfortunately.

MD: *Do you resent the powers–that–be who intervened to deny you?*

DD-L: It is pointless to resent. It just perpetrates a situation of malcontent. I was saddened not to be able to go there and I hope that some opportunity will be provided at a later date. Hopefully, those who have the power to make the decision will see that there is not an altogether frivolous reason for us going in there.

MD: *Getting back to your recent film, is there a danger that the merits of* In the Name of the Father *will be lost, particularly in England, where the tabloids have been bleating very loudly about the film being 'a paean to the IRA'? Emma Thompson got something of a hammering despite the fact that no journalist had even seen any rushes of the film.*

DD-L: I know, I know, that was amazing. It is a case of Chinese whispers. I think it is quite likely that we'll get a degree of adverse criticism and it's quite likely to come from people who know absolutely nothing about the film. If people see the film and really allow themselves to watch it objectively and then criticise it, fair enough. But a lot of criticism will come from quarters where people will already have made up their minds. It's true to say that in England there is a proportion of the population who would choose to believe, now, that the Guildford Four are still guilty and I doubt very much if our film will do anything to change their minds. Maybe some of the press will represent these people. I hope not but I am prepared for it. Already there is a tendency to regard the film as if it has some sort of leaning towards, you know, Republicanism, or some anarchic attitude about British justice, or some mindless criticism about police procedures, and so on. None of these things is true. None of these things.

MD: *There is a lot of pressure involved in your chosen profession, in the intense work you do and in having to do promotional tours. Was there ever a time, say when you were knee–deep in a freezing river wearing nothing but a loin cloth, when you felt, 'I wish I had stayed a cabinet–maker?'*

DD-L: Most days, yes! I was a hopeless businessman, but I'd have made a good journeyman cabinet-maker. Yeah, I'd have been OK. But when I made the initial decision, and again it was a decision that made itself, I had two fairly thoroughly formed misconceptions of those worlds — the serene world of the cabinet-maker as opposed to the neurotic world of theatre, and so on. Most of my preconceptions about the theatre are unfounded and, I suppose, most of those about cabinet-making would have been if I had allowed them to be. As I've never really developed that side of things, I probably still think of it as some sort of ideal.

MD: *So if a script came in and the opening direction read, "Interior: Cabinet–Makers: Morning", would that be the ideal compromise?*

DD-L: Oh, no way! I could never combine the two things! That would open the last door on my privacy and I could never imagine doing that!

POSTSCRIPT

Daniel Day–Lewis's next screen project will be a leading role in Arthur Miller's The Crucible, *adapted by the playwright himself. Otherwise, watch out for him pursuing one of his favourite hobbies, spinning around the Wicklow hills on his Harley Davidson.*

MOVIEGUIDE'S 10 FAVOURITE SCREEN BADDIES

1 "By what right do you interfere in the King's justice?" Basil Rathbone as Sir Guy of Gisbourne, *The Adventures of Robin Hood* (1938).

2 "Do you know what I do to squealers? I let 'em have it, right in the belly!" Richard Widmark as sniggering Tommy Udo, *Kiss of Death* (1947).

3 "Prove it!" Jack Palance as the gunfighter Wilson, *Shane* (1953).

4 "Thrall me with your acumen." Anthony Hopkins as Hannibal Lecter, *The Silence of the Lambs* (1991).

5 "Is it safe?" Laurence Olivier as Der Weisse Engel, *Marathon Man* (1976).

6 "I don't really care about what you know or don't know. I'm gonna torture you for a while, regardless." Michael Madsen, Mr Blond in *Reservoir Dogs* (1992).

7 "Shall I tell you the little story of Right-Hand/Left-Hand, the tale of Good and Evil?" Robert Mitchum as the Preacher, *The Night of the Hunter* (1955).

8 "Funny, how? I mean, funny like I'm a clown? I amuse you? I make you laugh?" Joe Pesci as Tommy DeVito, *GoodFellas* (1990).

9 "Wish you was a wishing well so I could tie a bucket to you and sink you." James Cagney as Tom Powers, *The Public Enemy* (1931).

10

"The truth is you're wanting, and you can't play in the man's game."
Alec Baldwin (below) as the guy from head office, *Glengarry Glen
Ross* (1993)

TAKE TEN FRANK McGUINNESS

*The section in which various personalities have been given three minutes to answer ten questions about their cinema-going habits. Next up is lecturer and playwright, Frank McGuinness (*Observe the Sons of Ulster...*, Bag Lady, Someone Who'll Watch Over Me).*

1 *If you were to be stranded on a desert island with nothing but a VCR and three films, what titles would you choose?*

Some Like It Hot (Wilder; 1959, US), *La Strada* (Fellini; 1954, It.) and *The Company of Wolves* (Jordan; 1987, Irl.)

2 *What was the most recent film you saw and how would you rate it out of ten?*

Four Weddings and a Funeral. The funeral, I'd give ten; the weddings, four.

3 *When was the last time you cried at the movies?*

At *Five Easy Pieces*, when Jack Nicholson's character tries to talk to his father — brilliant performances from both actors. The tears were tripping me up and I didn't realise it until the scene was finished.

4 *Who is the finest actor or actress you have ever seen?*

I worked in the theatre with Kelly McGillis and she is as good on stage as she is on film. Stephen Rea excels at both, as well. I'd watch Spencer Tracy in anything, and Meryl Streep is a great actress.

5 *Which figure do you most admire in Irish cinema?*

Neil Jordan, because he is a wonderful writer and, for all his success, he is still a modest, courteous and entertaining man.

6 *What is your attitude to sub-titles?*

European films are better than Hollywood films. Too many American films are rubbish — commercialised, censored or conservative. Billy Wilder is the only genius American cinema has ever produced — and he is from Vienna.

7   *What musical film can you sing in its entirety?*

The King and I, a favourite. And Yul Brynner is beautiful.

8   *Who is the actor or actress who most makes you want to throw your popcorn at the screen in disgust?*

Actors — the vast majority of them — have a very hard life and most earn very little money. They are the most dedicated people to their profession that I know. I mean that. If I've popcorn to spare, I'll throw it at the critics.

9   *If Hollywood were planning to film the story of your life, who would you like to see in the title role?*

What a lovely question. I've thought about it for ages, but of course, the answer is obvious: Julia Roberts.

10   *And what would it be called?*

My Nights with Lyle Lovett. Strictly Over 18s.

STACKS OF STYLE

Barbara Stanwyck

Almost forgotten in the pantheon of star actresses, Barbara Stanwyck (or 'Missy' as she was known to her friends) was undoubtedly one of the greats. Her popularity in the Forties was such that in 1944 the US Treasury listed her as the nation's top female money earner. (At $400,000 per annum, she even had the edge on Bette Davis.) Born Ruby Stevens in Brooklyn to a family of Irish and Scottish extraction, Barbara Stanwyck arrived in Hollywood via the vaudeville stage and was quick to make her mark. Though she felt that the secret of her success was her eyes, her greatest asset was the diversity of her acting approach as evinced in the variety of her Oscar-nominated roles – *Sorry Wrong Number* (1948), *Double Indemnity* (1944), *Ball of Fire* (1941) and her breakthrough performance, *Stella* ("I got stacks of style") *Dallas* (1937).

A typical performance by the more mature Stanwyck occurred in *Forty Guns* (1957) in which she played tough gal Jessica Drummond: "I was bitten by a rattler when I was 15," she tells co-star Barry O'Sullivan at one point. "I'll bet the rattler died," he replies. Though 50, Stanwyck threw herself into the part and insisted on performing a difficult stunt – where she is dragged by her horse – three times until she was satisfied.

A busy actress, later in her career Stanwyck turned to television, scooping Emmys for *The Barbara Stanwyck Show, The Big Valley* and *The Thorn Birds*. Her control on screen (both big and small) continued to pervade her performances. "Working with Barbara Stanwyck was one of the greatest pleasures of my career," said Fritz Lang, who directed the actress in *Clash by Night* (1952). "She's fantasic, unbelievable and I liked her tremendously." And the secret to that control was her preparation: "I must learn the entire script for a film," she once explained, "exactly as I would a stage play. Then I don't care where the director goes because I know everything."

For Barbara Stanwyck, like Phyllis Dietrichson, it was always "straight down the line".

THE PICK OF STANWYCK

Double Indemnity (1944)
"I wonder if you wonder." *Femme fatale* Phyllis is the jewel in Stanwyck's acting crown. The blonde hair, the ankle bracelet and a caustic script by Billy Wilder and Raymond Chandler. What chance did Fred MacMurray have?

Meet John Doe (1941)
A feast of Capra corn as newspaperwoman Stanwyck turns Gary Cooper into the epitome of everyday America only to see him exploited by nasty politician Edward Arnold. One of five films to team Capra and Stanwyck (the others being *Ladies of Leisure, The Miracle Woman, Forbidden,* and *The Bitter Tea of General Yen*).

The Lady Eve (1941)
"A moonlit deck is a woman's business office." Card sharp Stanwyck shows her skill at playing screwball comedy as she attempts to separate millionaire Henry Fonda from the contents of his wallet. *The Lady Eve* also boasts a superb supporting cast including Eugene Pallette and Charles Coburn ("It certainly took you a long time to come back in the same outfit").

THE SIX-MILLION-DOLLAR WOMAN

The Four Seasons Hotel in Beverly Hills is accustomed to celebrity. In fact, it's the sort of place where the clientele tend to be either very, very rich or very, very famous, or both. Looking around the vast and salubrious foyer, one can only imagine the roll call of stars who have darkened its towels over the years. Today, however, all the attention is focused on an actress who was virtually unknown 12 months ago.

In Hollywood parlance, Sandra Bullock is hot. Red hot. After co-starring with Keanu Reeves in the $120 million–grossing Speed in summer 1994, she recently toplined the romantic comedy While You Were Sleeping to an impressive $50 million in its first month of release. As a result, she has gone from nowhere to the very top of the A–list.

Lean, elegant and a vision in white, the 28–year–old actress greets me with a disarming "Hi, I'm Sandy!", leaps into her seat opposite and betrays no sign of her newly elevated status. In fact, Sandra Bullock seems genuinely surprised by her own success.

"I've been working non-stop since *Speed* came out so I have no idea what the reaction is of people out there," she says. "I don't think you can ever know exactly what people think, anyway. I used to really worry about what other people thought but, once I began to get my feelings hurt a lot, I said to myself, `You've got to get over it', and so I kind of isolated myself. I have a great network of friends I've known over the years. I just work and I go home and I play with the people I was playing with as a kid."

The story of Sandra Bullock's rise to fame is the closest real life has ever come to the celebrated *A Star Is Born* scenario. The girl from Arlington, Virginia, waited tables in New York, and appeared in a dodgy television series (*Working Girl*) before starting her film career with the B-movie king, Roger Corman (*Fire on the Amazon*). There is one

telling difference, however. Where Esther Blodgett was forced to ditch her cumbersome name in favour of the more exotic Vicki Lester, Sandra Bullock has retained her moniker. It is a typical gesture from this strong-willed daughter of a German soprano and a vocal coach from Alabama, who had enough belief in herself to persevere in one of the most difficult professions of all.

"I knew all the time that I would get work as an actress," she explains. "I just never thought it would be on this scale! Never in a million years did I think a bus movie would open every door that I possibly wanted! You know that you are going to have to pound the pavement in the beginning. It's an industry. You fight for your parts and you know that they are going to want names. I totally understand that. I never started out with a set list of directors I wanted to work with. I hoped that there was a director who could pull things out of me that another one couldn't. Whether it was a first-time director like Jan De Bont (*Speed*), or Jon Turtletaup (*While You Were Sleeping*), who has exactly the same sense of humour as me."

This is the same Jon Turtletaup who, while discussing Sandra Bullock prior to the interview, had described her as someone "you don't know whether you want to make love to or play poker with". Having considered both options, I had to admit that personally, I would not be bothering the woman with talk of straight flushes and jacks to open. In fact, meeting Sandra Bullock has a strange effect on the interviewer. You start out reminding yourself that she's a Hollywood star and you're a journalist assigned to do a professional job. You say to yourself that behind the beautiful exterior there probably lurks an ego-massaged actress, surrounded by a coterie of yes-men.

That's the theory. The reality is a little different. After five minutes I was warming to her obvious charm. After fifteen minutes, I marvelled

at her endearing self-effacement, and, by the time we got halfway through the interview, I just wanted to bring her home to meet my mother.

So it goes with Sandra Bullock, yet the actress who took the Most Desirable Female Award (ahead of Sharon and Demi) at the MTV Movie Awards, finds it hard to accept herself as an object of adulation.

"I don't think people look at me and go, oh boy, I think I'll get her in the sack!" she offers. "I don't think I have that vibe. I have more of a funny, kooky vibe."

This funny, kooky vibe emerges in full during *While You Were Sleeping*, a Capra-esque tale in which she plays a woman hooked on comatose Peter Gallagher while finding herself the object of his brother, Bill Pullman's, affections. If *Speed* got her noticed, *While You Were Sleeping* has made her a superstar. In fact, from start to finish, the film is a paean to the actress, filled with long, lingering close-ups.

"When I first saw *While You Were Sleeping*, I had no opinion whatsoever," Sandra recalls. "I have never had to watch myself so much! Usually when I watch a film I'm in four scenes and I get to enjoy the rest of the film and say, 'Here comes my scene!' With this film I was saying, 'Enough already with my face!'"

The more you listen to Sandra Bullock, the more you realise that her down-to-earth lifestyle is not something which has been concocted by a PR guru. She likes listening to Tom Jones records, goes ballroom dancing three nights a week, likes rock climbing, enjoys producing plays with her friends at Mr Otto's Barking Theatre, and has a soft spot for Dr Seuss.

"I'm a basic person. I have simple tastes," the actress explains. "I like things that I understand, things that I can identify and not have to question their motives. My friends are brutally honest, my parents are brutally honest. You always know where you stand and you never allow yourself to be set up for disappointments later on. I have a great place to live and go to work. My friends love what I do and they come and visit me where I do it. I share it all with my friends and family." No surprise then that

when she got her first big pay cheque, she went straight out and bought a BMW for her parents before heading off with her friends on a holiday.

"Things like limousines intimidate me," she continues. "I don't do well at flashy parties because most of the people there are people who aren't my friends. The people that you work with; it's a business. You go to these things because it's a work thing, but I work all day so I'd rather have a barbecue at my house and a pool tournament."

With her recent success, Sandra Bullock will find it increasingly difficult to find time for barbecues and pool tournaments. The actress is currently starring in the computer thriller *The Net,* and will then co-star with Dennis Leary in *Two If By Sea.* That will be followed by the costume drama *Kate and Leopold,* and, finally, the big one, John Grisham's latest thriller, *A Time to Kill,* for which the actress will pocket six million dollars. Not that she is motivated by the lucre.

"The money is great. But if you are just doing it for the money you are going to sink rather quickly," she says. "Look at anybody who has ever done things just for money. I'd rather do it for the fun. I've got plenty of money, I don't need any more! I'm really only interested in the script and I have been lucky to find a lot of good scripts. We have had strong actresses over the past five or six years who have forged a great path for us. Julia Roberts, Demi Moore, Meryl Streep, Jessica Lange, Susan Sarandon — they all paved the way. We are reaping the benefits because they cannot do all the films. I don't look at parts and go, 'I'll do it, it's a huge role.' Everybody else who read the part for *Speed* passed on it because they felt it wasn't something they could play with. I look at the play aspect of roles; if I'm going to have a really good time doing it, maybe my work will be that much better or that much different."

And this is not just talk. Sandra Bullock has put her principles on the line, threatening to quit the business on two occasions.

"I almost quit twice," she confirms, "only because I sat there and realised that things are way beyond your control in this industry. It's not like if you study harder you will become smarter and get a better job. That has nothing to do with it. I just didn't find myself living a fulfilling life and I felt that I had no hand in making my career go, so I said that I would give myself until the end of the year (1992). All the scripts that were coming in were cheesy and pretty bad. I wasn't going to do a beach film because nobody wants to see me in a bikini and it wasn't funny. I gave myself until the end of the year and in that year, I got two roles on the same day (*The Vanishing, The Thing Called Love*)."

Of course, for a woman who almost quit, and who fully understands the fickle nature of fame, Sandra Bullock has bravely turned down two coveted roles, *Batman Forever* (step up Nicole Kidman) and *Sabrina* (enter Julia Ormond). But that is the essence of the woman. She's open, she's honest, and she doesn't mind telling you that since the break-up with actor Tate Donovan (her co-star in *Love Potion Number Nine*) she has often been lonely. "I just want somebody to brush my hair and tuck me into bed," she told one paper. "I'm convinced I will never find the right person," she confided to another.

POSTSCRIPT

If you don't find him soon, Sandra, the offer still stands and my mother would love to meet you.

MOVIEGUIDE'S 10 FAVOURITE BRIEF (BUT TELLING) MOVIE MOMENTS

1 The moment in *The Postman Always Rings Twice* (Tay Garnett, 1946) when Lana Turner and John Garfield are first introduced via a lipstick tube that has rolled between them.

2 The moment in *Strangers On a Train* (Alfred Hitchcock, 1951) when the entire audience at a tennis match is following the ball as it criss-crosses the net, save for Robert Walker, who is gazing fixedly at Farley Granger.

3 The moment in *On The Waterfront* (Elia Kazan, 1954) when an awkward Marlon Brando is trying to explain his feelings for Eva Marie Saint. She drops her white gloves and he (apparently unrehearsed) picks one up and puts it on his hand.

4 The moment in *Ace in the Hole* (Billy Wilder, 1951) when cynical journalist Kirk Douglas demonstrates how to strike a match off the rolling barrel of a typewriter.

5 The scene in *Once Upon a Time in the West* (Sergio Leone, 1969) when tough guy Jack Elam becomes frustrated by the attentions of a fly.

6 The moment in *The Deer Hunter* (Michael Cimino, 1978) when Robert De Niro awkwardly goes to kiss Meryl Streep at a wedding party only to pull back in embarrassment at the last moment.

7 The moment in *The Searchers* (John Ford, 1956) when Ward Bond spies Martha stroking John Wayne's jacket and realises that there was once a strong bond between brother and sister-in-law.

8   The moment in *Lawrence of Arabia* [David Lean, 1962] when, through slick editing, Peter O'Toole's blowing-out of a match is immediately followed by a blazing Arabian sunset.

9   The moment in *Blood Simple* [Joel Coen, 1984] when John Getz and Amy Madigan come to a sudden realisation about a murder and their silence is shattered by a newspaper hammering against the door.

10   The scene in *Once Upon a Time in America* [Sergio Leone, 1984] when DeNiro has returned to his gang, to discover that James Woods is now leader (and sitting on a throne). Everyone wants to see how he will react. DeNiro simply asks for a cup of coffee and, as the tension gathers, begins stirring, and stirring, and stirring...

Turner and Garfield ignore the postman's knock.

THE MADNESS AND THE METHOD

Marlon Brando

Recent film audiences are chiefly aware of Marlon Brando through the lurid tabloid headlines following the tragedies in his family, or the wags who make comments about his imposing girth. The fact remains, however, that of all the actors who have ever appeared before a camera, Marlon Brando is the finest. After a brief but telling stage career, the Omaha-born actor burst onto the scene in the Fifties with a string of roles — *The Men, A Streetcar Named Desire, Viva Zapata!, Julius Caesar, The Wild One* — which provided him with a clutch of Oscar nominations before *On the Waterfront* and Terry Molloy finally landed him the statuette.

The importance of Brando to his peers is immense. His naturalist style, steeped in the Stanislavsky Method, liberated actors to talk and act as the people they saw around

them ("I guess I must strike you as the unrefined type," says Stanley in *Streetcar*). Meanwhile, those critics who saw him as little more than a mumbler were answered by his articulate portrayal of Mark Antony in *Julius Caesar*.

During the Sixties, through a mixture of poor choices and indifference to his art ("Acting is an empty and useless profession") Brando failed to capitalise on his success, though he did prove his directing skills with the excellent western *One Eyed Jacks* in 1961. In the Seventies, he provided the occasional reminder of his class, notably with *The Godfather*, *Last Tango in Paris* and *Apocalypse Now*, all of which had moments of sublime brilliance, but it was poor return for such a talent.

Marlon Brando may have occasionally given himself a one-way ticket to Palookaville, but he was never just a contender, he was always the champ.

THE PICK OF BRANDO

A Streetcar Named Desire (1951)
Brando as the brutish Stanley Kowalksi turned screen acting on its head with a visceral, powerhouse performance which has yet to be bettered on film. There is superb acting all round in Elia Kazan's film, from Kim Hunter's Stella to Vivien Leigh's Oscar-winning Blanche, but this is Brando's film and few will forget the sight of him standing at the bottom of the stairs in that wet, torn t-shirt, bellowing, "Stella! Hey Stella!"

On the Waterfront (1954)
Brando's first Oscar-winning role as the ex-pug Terry Molloy who "could've been a contender" was another revelatory performance. Director Kazan claimed it was the best he ever witnessed and there is certainly plenty to admire: Brando and Eva Marie Saint going through an awkward courtship ("You grew up real nice"), Brando bemoaning the death of his beloved pigeons, and, of course, Brando and Steiger in the back of the taxi-cab: "It wasn't him, it was you, Charlie."

The Godfather (1972)

They were writing off the big man as a has-been following a string of indifferent films, but Brando reminded us why he is considered the greatest with a superb performance as the ageing Don Corleone, controlling the fortunes of his family. We knew he was tough enough ("If you had come to me in friendship, then this scum that ruined your daughter would be suffering this very day") but there was a strong, sensitive streak on offer, too, notably in the scene where Robert Duvall informs him of Sonny's death.

AN AUSTRIAN IN PARIS

Paris on a sunny Tuesday afternoon. High above the Champs-Elysees, on the terrace of an exclusive hotel, the world's biggest movie star is getting ready to meet selected members of the European press corps. Down below, the beautiful people are slowly boulevarding, stopping here and there to sip the occasional *café au lait* and scoop the odd Haagen-Dazs (or two). It's that kind of a day. Two pm. The appointed time for the Schwarzenegger interview and, typically, the man is bang on time. "Hold the pose, keep the stomach in," jokes a familiar, heavily accented voice to a security guard, now clearly regretting his almost involuntary flexing in front of the body builder *du jour*. At six foot two inches and with a torso that would put your average brick outhouse to shame, Arnie is capable of quite an entrance. He wears a polo shirt and

jeans, and his handshake is firm and the greeting earnest as he settles down to his glass of Evian and the almost obligatory giant Cuban cigar which has become the actor's leitmotif.

Arnie is in the City of Light to promote his latest film, *The Last Action Hero,* an adventure about a young boy (Austin O'Brien) who finds himself magically transported into his idol's (our Austrian friend's) newest action film. It is a slight departure from the actor's recent cocktail of comedy and violence which has elevated Graz's most famous son to the very height of his profession, from where, at the age of 45, he commands ten million dollars (and the odd Lear jet) per film.

"When I was young and watching movies," explains the actor when asked why he should have signed up for *The Last Action Hero* and not the two dozen other scripts which are posted to his agent each day, "I always wanted to be up on the screen with John Wayne. Or I would have liked him to ride out of the screen and be part of the real world. At the same time, this film was a good way of looking at my life, the movies I have done in the past, mostly action films, and having some fun with that. It is no different than being able to laugh at anything you do. I am sure that you will be able to laugh at your job, travelling around, meeting movie guys and going to films.

"That's funny! Being a body builder and standing there with the posing trunks on, that's funny!"

Having seen *The Last Action Hero* and monitored the response of fans and critics in the States, I have the impression that not too many people are getting the joke. For the first time, the master calculator, who has successfully reinvented himself at key times in his career, from monosyllabic muscle man to wisecracking tough guy to comedy foil, would appear to have stepped out of kilter with his audience.

Or is it that the media has a hidden agenda when it comes to Schwarzenegger these days? Is he a classic victim of his own success? Or is the film simply a big let-down? The actor takes a big pull on his cigar before answering with almost alarming conviction.

"There is a hidden agenda from the outset, because Hollywood never likes films about Hollywood.

They always attack films that look behind the scenes. Secondly, you are absolutely right: when you have four or five movies in a row that were hits, as mine were, and make over a billion dollars, you are ripe for attack. The press in the States, especially, like to take you on a rollercoaster ride; one year they build you up, the next year they tear you down.

"Look what happened to Bill Clinton. He was billed as the Saviour, yet three months into his administration, the press started beating him up. That's the way it is with this film but I can't complain about it and I never will. I got a great ride from the press. They always looked at me as the great American success story; the guy coming over with nothing and making it to the top. I know that eventually when you make it to the top, you are going to be torn down. Before they even saw this movie they talked about test screenings that never happened, saying there were budget problems etc. There never was a budget problem. The only people who would have a problem are the studio heads and they were smiling all the way. There was no problem so the media created a problem."

As he delivers his considered and measured responses to every question, Schwarzenegger has an intensity about him which is uncommon in nearly all of his peers. He fixes his interrogator with a steady gaze which suggests, as one writer put it, "that any question which might ruffle Schwarzenegger's serenity will be rewarded with unspeakable retribution".

In reality, it has to be said that Arnie is the model interviewee; he listens to every word and appears deeply interested in every question (hell, he is not a good enough actor to fake it). Quite an achievement for a man who conducted 50 interviews per day at the recent Cannes Film Festival. Where other actors treat press interviews as a contractually necessary evil, Schwarzenegger thrives on the experience and seldom lets his guard down. Indeed he refuses to be ruffled when I suggest that the studio might be disappointed with their return on *The Last Action Hero* if early box-office is any indication. He regards the putative showdown with Spielberg's dinosaurs as a media invention and is quite happy to discuss the financial gains which the film will accrue (at times like these you are reminded that Arnie has a business degree from the University of Wisconsin).

"Those comments about the film losing money show you how stupid this kind of stuff is," he explains. Columbia Pictures got $20 million to make the action dolls. They got $28 million from the video rights, $60 million from theatre owners in the US, in advance. That takes you over $100 million and the picture cost $64 million, so I would say that they are already smiling. It wasn't important to them that they open bigger than *Jurassic Park* or anything like that. What was more important was the long-term effect.

"One third of the income from all my pictures is in the US, two thirds from the overseas markets. Every movie I choose I will approach on a global level, not just what I see in the United States. I was born overseas, I am a foreigner and I always look to see how my films do overseas. When the dust is settled and everything is done, that's when judgement day comes."

And who would bet against Arnie come the day of judgement? For a body-builder to arrive from the village of Graz in Austria and work his way up to movie stardom without even shedding his accent (or being overburdened with acting ability) is quite an achievement. Naturalised as a US citizen in 1983, the actor is married to Maria Schriver, TV star and scion of the Kennedy clan. Yet despite being the epitome of the American Dream, who had the friendship of one President (Bush) and the respect of another (Clinton), Schwarzenegger is intensely proud of his European upbringing.

When some tabloid hacks, as is their wont, picked up on the fact that *vater* Schwarzenegger was a police chief in a small Austrian town, and made all sorts of Nazi-related claims, Arnie struck back. In a highly publicised court case, the actor won an action against Wendy Leigh, author of an unauthorised biography of the actor which claimed to have proof of this contentious link. Now that the dust is settled, the actor is happy to broach the subject, thus refuting the

suggestion of some journalists who have said that to mention the word "Nazi" in the big man's presence is to invite, at the very least, an eye of the darkest hue.

"I was very satisfied with the outcome of that court case because, as you know, I never complain about anything anybody writes about me because it is all one's opinion," he says, adjusting his position so he is in direct eye contact again. "If someone says I am a terrible actor, that's his opinion. If someone says he loves the movie, that's his opinion. People should write whatever they want and so be it.

"But if someone goes out, like Wendy Leigh did, and writes something which gets heavily picked up by the Austrian press, that really pisses me off. Calling me a Nazi and saying that my father killed Jews and homosexuals in the Second World War and that I do Hitler salutes before lunch and all that crap, that's different. I felt this was the time when I had to strike out and sue. First of all to win back the right of my father, who is dead, and also for myself. Finally now, after all these years, she admitted that she made

mistakes, that stuff was totally untrue, and she had to go to court to apologise and pay the money."

Arnold Schwarzenegger is a success because he knows his own limitations and strengths. He doesn't need the press or people within the industry telling him how or why he clicks with the public. He is a self-publicist *non pareil* whose health and fitness campaigns have complemented his on-screen heroic persona. Ask him why he, and not any one of the legions of musclebound Arnie wannabees, should have made it to the top of the heap, however, and he becomes rather coy.

"We don't make ourselves get to the top," says the actor, pausing to relight the hefty cigar. "What you see in front of you is absolutely nothing without the people. The only thing that makes a star is the people. We're totally reliant on that. If you are successful it is because you are doing things that people want to see. The kind of movies you do, the characters that you play, the type of life you lead, the body-building, the fitness promotion. Whatever it is, it seems to click. I don't do surveys on these things. I would just say it's the whole package. That's why people go to the movies, that's why I am where I am today. It is not much to do with me other than the fact that I supply the things that people want to see."

Three pm. Interview over and it's back out to the Champs-Elysées. Arnie has repaired to the roof-top for a final photo call. A young couple pause at the spectacle of a large gent surrounded by exploding flash bulbs. After a few seconds they decide that he must be an innocuous male model unworthy of their attention, so they move on.

Quel dommage.

REEL 4

TALES
OF
HOFFMAN

"Listen, you have to hear this joke that Steve Martin told me!"
The scene is a plush hotel room in London. An extremely
animated Dustin Hoffman is leaping out of his seat, anxious to
relate the one about the amorous flea, the elephant and the
coconut. Indeed, the disposition of the double Oscar-winner is
such that one wonders if reports of Hoffman's legendary gravitas
have been greatly exaggerated.

Hoffman is in London to promote Accidental Hero, *a big-*
budget flick directed by Stephen Frears and co-starring Geena
Davis and Andy Garcia. Despite the presence of such luminaries,
however, the film failed to make much of an impact on the US
box-office. Still, Hoffman is in good form and confident that
European audiences might react a little more favourably. Dressed
casually in baggy cords and a blue shirt, he is tanned, lean, and

as short as you would expect, and the only visible sign of wear and tear is a dash of grey at the temples.

Throughout the interview, Hoffman continues in an animated vein. As he describes early films in his career, he is up out of his seat, demonstrating how one scene worked and why another could have worked better. During these moments, he employs the interviewer as a sort of foil. One moment I'm Jon Voight in Midnight Cowboy, *the next I'm Jessica Lange in* Tootsie. *Here is an actor who, despite having being, for 28 years, one of the greatest stars in the business with hits ranging from* All the President's Men *to* The Graduate, *still gets excited about his chosen profession.*

<u>Michael Doherty:</u>

You have just made four films back–to–back which is unusual for you, looking back over your career. Was that a conscious effort to be busier on your part, or was it just that these particular scripts leapt out at you?

<u>Dustin Hoffman:</u>

It is unusual for me and I suppose that it was an experiment that I was doing. I had just finished *Rain Man* after a year and a half of preparation and I just said, 'Enough of this'. DeNiro, Nicholson, Hackman, they're all making lots of movies. Depardieu, God knows, he's younger than me and he's done about a hundred movies! He has no life. He must go to sleep right there on the sound stage! After *Rain Man*, I did three days on *Dick Tracy*, then *The Merchant of Venice* on stage, then straight to *Billy Bathgate,* then on to *Hook,* and now *Hero.*

At this stage, I'm finished with that experiment and I won't do it again!

MD: *The character of Bernie LaPlante in* Accidental Hero *[a small-time hoodlum who becomes a hero when he rescues reporter Geena Davis from a crashed plane], bears more than a passing resemblance to Ratso Rizzo from* Midnight Cowboy. *Was it difficult not to turn the role into Ratso Returns?*

DH: I had long talks with the director and the writer about this very subject. We all sat around and said, "What are the differences between Ratso and Bernie?" There are similarities in the same way that there are similarities between Clinton and Jimmy Carter. They are both liberals, they are both Democrats, they are both from the South. At a certain point, however, they diverge. Bernie and Ratso: if you are an actor playing those parts, you don't want to keep the wardrobe at the end of the movie, that's one similarity! They are also both fringe characters, anti-social figures, though Ratso is in the gutter and Bernie is on the kerb. To me, that was the end of the similarities. Ratso is a survivor, he has an ambition, he is dangerous. If he meets Bernie he eats him for breakfast. Bernie can't see beyond today, he has no peripheral vision and no dreams for the future. Ratso would not have gone near that airplane. And that's the difference.

MD: *What attracts you to playing such characters as Bernie, Ratso and Raymond from* Rainman?

DH: I can't do a character unless I like him. And it's funny, I read an interview with DeNiro recently, and he said the same thing. I don't think you can do a character unless you like them because I think that every human being rationalises their own flaws and weaknesses. We all live with an essential lie about ourselves. We all distort ourselves in order to get through life because we are not heroes, we are flawed. God messed up! If He did it properly, we wouldn't be destroying the planet right now! But then again, maybe He didn't mess up. Maybe He is saying, "It was the women who were supposed to have all the power." Then everything would have been all right!

MD: *Looking back over your career, it's clear that* Tootsie *was a very important movie in your life...*

DH: I would like to do nothing but make films like *Tootsie* for the rest of my life. *Tootsie* was an idea which arose when my friend asked me: "What if you were a woman? Would your personality change? And how?" This is a profound question and my first answer was, "It depends what I looked like", because how I looked had so much to do with how I developed as a man.

MD: *How so?*

DH: I was skinny and small. The girls did not find me attractive. I wasn't Troy Donahue, I wasn't Tab Hunter, I wasn't Robert Redford. For *Tootsie*, we did make-up tests for six months. I got Ann-Margret's wigs. "Make me as beautiful as possible," I said, expecting to be transformed into a beautiful woman. Finally, when we put rushes on the screen, I looked up and said, "Yes, now I look like a woman. Now make me look beautiful." And they said, "That's it. That's as good as it gets." That was a lesson for me. I knew that I was an interesting person. I liked my intelligence; I liked my wit; I liked my *joie de vivre* as this woman Dorothy. But I knew that if I, as a man, had come into a party and seen me as a woman, I would not have approached me. That made me more emotional than any part I have ever done.

MD: *Accidental Hero is a film which explores the cult of celebrity and the role of media in hero creation. Who would be your own heroes?*

DH: For some reason, even though I had no thought of becoming an actor at the time, John Garfield was an early hero of mine. Maybe it was because he was short! When I was five or six I saw *The Yearling* with Gregory Peck and he became my quintessential father figure. Joe Louis was another great hero of mine and, as I got older, Muhammad Ali also became a hero, and he still is.

MD: *Why Ali?*

DH: I cannot think of any other professional in my lifetime who sincerely gave up the best years of his professional life for something he believed in. He was philosophically against the killing of other people. His most famous line was "No Viet Cong ever called me nigger." He was one of the greatest athletes of all time yet we never saw him at his best. And that is chilling!

MD: *You have a reputation as a 'difficult' actor. Do you deserve it?*

DH: My reputation for being difficult has been distorted. There are far more 'difficult' actors in the business, that we all know, but their experiences are not written about. Warren Beatty is the Womaniser. Jack Nicholson is, well, Jack. I am the Difficult One and it goes on and on. What is the truth? The truth is that Warren Beatty didn't get laid more times than Jack Nicholson. Many movie stars who had the power had men and women available to them, but Warren gets the badge. Or Jack with drugs. Everybody took drugs in the Seventies and Jack probably took less than other actors. I have made something like 24 films, had only three or four difficult experiences, and I cannot remember the label before *Tootsie*. Sydney Pollack and I had difficulties on the picture but we never fought in front of the crew and I have never fought with anybody in my life. It was always a difference of opinion over the script, but you have to remember, in addition to being the lead actor on the film, I was also the producer. It was my project and had been for three years. Most people don't realise that. I don't have a publicist and maybe that's been my problem all along!

POSTSCRIPT

Since Accidental Hero, *Dustin Hoffman has enjoyed one of the biggest box-office successes of his career with Wolfgang Petersen's* Outbreak. *Hoffman took over the lead role when Harrison Ford pulled out.*

MOVIEGUIDE'S 10 FAVOURITE ROMANTIC MOMENTS

1 "Forbid me ever to leave you." Jean Simmons to Kirk Douglas, *Spartacus* (1960)

2 "Now I've kissed you through two centuries." Laurence Olivier embracing Vivien Leigh as the bells chime midnight on New Year's Eve, 1799, *Lady Hamilton* (1941)

3 "You grew up real nice." Marlon Brando to Eva Marie Saint, *On the Waterfront* (1954)

4 "He says it's the chance of a lifetime." Donna Reed, James Stewart and a shared phone call, *It's a Wonderful Life* (1946)

5 "You know what's after happening, don't you?" Trevor Howard to Celia Johnson, *Brief Encounter* (1945)

6 "I've never been so miserable in all my life as I have been since I met you. But I wouldn't trade a minute of it." Burt Lancaster to Deborah Kerr, *From Here to Eternity* (1953)

7 "Walking through life with you, ma'am, has been a very gracious thing, indeed." Errol Flynn's Custer taking leave of Olivia De Havilland, *They Died With Their Boots On* (1941)

8 "If all men knew that banishment would be like this, we'd have a world of exiles." Charlton Heston to Sophia Loren, *El Cid* (1961)

9 "I always make you mad, John T, don't I? Well then, don't let me tell you why I stayed." Angie ('Feathers') Dickinson to John Wayne, *Rio Bravo* (1959)

10 "Marry me, Emily, and I'll never look at any other horse." Er, Groucho to Margaret Dumont, *A Day at the Races* (1937)

OSCAR BRAVO

Throughout its 67-year history, the Academy of Motion Pictures Arts and Sciences has only occasionally proferred its highest honour, the Oscar, on an Irish member of the film industry.

From Greer Garson to Josie McAvin to Neil Jordan, Irish success has often been in isolation. The exceptions in this regard were the year *My Left Foot* shot to acclaim (1989), and, more particularly, 1994, when Jim Sheridan's *In the Name of the Father* garnered seven nominations.

Not surprisingly, Hollywood braced itself for the biggest Irish party Tinseltown had ever seen and Movieguide was there to capture it all...

A handful of protesters scream, "Repent movie idols, God's judgement is at hand!"; traffic in downtown LA is at a complete standstill; a plane circles overhead trailing a banner which reads, "World's greatest movie script needs producer – just call 074 203 5760". Yes folks, this can only be the annual Hollywood spectacle known as the Academy Awards.

For the 66th time, the great and the good of the film world have gathered to honour, well, themselves. For some of these famous faces gathering at the Dorothy Chandler Pavilion, the receipt of a 13-and-a-half-inch gold statuette will be little more than a nice conversation filler at parties; for others, it is a golden passport to first-read scripts, longer business lunches and, ultimately, a crack at the big time.

The flash-bulbs are popping, the television cameras are rolling and the necks of those in the bleachers are straining as the parade of seriously famous faces files by. On and on they come, each bearing gloriously blemish-free skin, gravity-defying cleavage and the confidence that only extremes of wealth and power can engender.

"I love you, Sharon!" screams an intrepid fan of Ms Stone from the upper branches of a tree overlooking the scene. "CHRISTIAN! Look over here, pleeeeze!" yells a teenage girl at The Man Who Would Be Jack Nicholson. "How are you doing?" drawls Mr Slater and another fan is destined for a sleepless night.

On and on they come, people who are known the world over by their first names — Al, Geena, Goldie, Glenn, Winona and Clint. The star couples are out in force, too. Tom and Nicole, Jeremy and Sinéad, Alec and Kim, Kurt and Goldie, Liam and Natasha. The sight of Ellen and Gabriel together sets the tongues wagging. The latter, in her gold Versace dress, earns the particular kudos of the assembled fashion scribes.

Amongst these designer-clad beautiful people, the *In the Name of the Father* troupe are taking it all in their stride. Don Baker and producer Arthur Lappin stroll over for a few words with a tuxedoed Movieguide,

while Jim Sheridan and his mum are doing the rounds of the television crews. And then he arrives: the man they have all come to honour. Steven Spielberg looks cool, calm and ready to collect. He is not going to be disappointed.

Backstage, as Whoopi sets things in motion, the awards are turning into a predictable procession. In recent weeks, there had been talk of a *Schindler* backlash (too documentary-like for Best Picture) and a *Piano* backlash (over-aggressive Oscar lobbying) but Steven, Holly and Jane duly arrive with Oscar in tow.

The only frisson of excitement occurs when Anna Paquin's name is read out. As the elfin Kiwi arrives backstage, the press distinguish themselves with the inanity of their questions: "How tall are you, Anna?" asks a New York reporter. "I don't know, " replies the pre-teen. "What projects and commitments have you made or lined up?" offers an LA hack. "Er, sorry?" replies the bemused and decidedly uncomfortable Oscar winner.

When the gold dust had settled and the stretch-limo drivers had put away their coffee and doughnuts, it was time to take stock of the evening's encomium hand-out. Spielberg, Hanks and Hunter were in raptures. The *In The Name of the Father*

crew, who batted 0 for 7, were disappointed, but headed off to Jimmy's to scoop the only remaining accolade — Best Post-Oscar Party.

At Jimmy's, the Murphiosi (including Colm Meaney) quaffed copious amounts of Guinness, downed plates of boiled beef and cabbage, and launched into a variety of Irish ballads. Elmer Bernstein and David Thewlis (who deserved an Oscar nomination for his searing performance in Mike Leigh's *Naked*) were also on hand to drown the shamrock.

At the end of the day, however, there was little to be despondent about. *In The Name of the Father* is heading for the $50 million mark in the US and Jim Sheridan is feted as a unique talent. In fact, a few days before the Oscars, one producer threw a Beverly Hills party in honour of the Dublin director and provided Movieguide with its most unforgettable moment of the Oscar trip. Among the luminaries gathered in this salubrious mansion were Jack Lemmon and Shirley MacLaine. In the middle of an interview with the latter, an earthquake tremor struck; the ground shook, and the guests scattered. Quite a sight.

En route to Jimmy's for the post-Oscar party, we passed the Vista Cinema on Sunset Boulevard. Two men were standing on ladders adding "Winner of Seven Oscars" to their *Schindler's List* marquee. It was 9.38, eight minutes after the finale of the Oscar telecast.

In Hollywood, it doesn't pay to waste time.

MOVIEGUIDE'S ALTERNATIVE ACADEMY AWARDS 1994

Most Surprised Winner: Anna Paquin

Most Disappointed Loser: Winona Ryder

Best Acceptance Comment: "I'd like to believe in God to thank him, but I just believe in Billy Wilder" — Fernando Trueba, director of Best Foreign Language Film, *Belle Epoque*

Best Backstage Comment: "Lady, I'm lucky to still have a pulse!" — Paul Newman, in response to why he still looks sexy at 69

Best Put-Down of a Silly Question: "You'll force me to revert to my character" — Holly Hunter, responding to a hack who implied that Hollywood invariably confers Oscars on actors that play mute roles

Most Disappointed Table of Hacks: The Taiwanese contingent, eight of whom had flown over to support *The Wedding Banquet*'s unsuccessful bid for Best Foreign Film

Least Helpful Press Information: The resident Oscar historian who declared to all hacks that Holly Hunter was the fourth person to win an Oscar in a non-speaking role, following Patty Duke (*The Miracle Worker*), Jane Wyman (*Johnny Belinda*) and Marlee Matlin (*Children of a Lesser God*). Have these people never seen John Mills in *Ryan's Daughter?*

Least Successful Entrepreneur: The chap selling t-shirts at the Dorothy Chandler Pavilion bearing the legend "OCSAR 94"

REEL 5

SUPERMODEL TO SILVERSCREEN

Thirty–five–year–old Andie McDowell was born and raised in South Carolina. One of the first supermodels to grace the fashion catwalks, she first hit our screens in Greystoke — The Legend of Tarzan *(an unhappy experience, since her voice was dubbed by Glenn Close) before making a huge impact with a leading role in Steven Soderbergh's Cannes–wooing* sex, lies and videotape *and a Golden Globe–winning performance opposite Gerard Depardieu in Peter Weir's* Green Card. *At the time of our interview, she was enjoying her biggest commercial success to date with* Groundhog Day, *co–starring Bill Murray.*

Andie MacDowell lives on a farm in Montana with her husband, former model Paul Qualley, and their two children.

Michael Doherty:

You were carving out a successful career as an international model. What made you decide to take up acting?

Andie MacDowell:

I was always interested in acting, even before the modelling. As a little girl I was always putting on performances and I remember walking miles for an audition. I've studied acting but college just wasn't something that was a reality for me. I mean I was going to get my degree in special education because, in my family growing up, women were told that they should have something to fall back on. My mother got her degree in education; my three sisters got their degrees in education. That's what I was going to do but I was bored. Fortunately, I was bad at school and had to take time off! It was during those times that I modelled. I never really thought of it as a career. It just sort of took off and all of sudden I was making all this money. I just couldn't believe it!

MD: *You met your husband around this time, also...*

AM: Yes, we met doing a fashion shoot for the Gap. I had never really been attracted to models, not because, as some people think, they are dumb or anything. The guys I usually chose were not that good looking, they were always more interesting and intelligent. When I saw him, that was that. I never had that happen before where, you know, you couldn't breathe, that sort of thing.

MD: *How do you balance your fame with your normal life as a wife and mother?*

AM: This was one of the frustrating things I had to deal with when I first became `famous'. I wanted to be normal, which was difficult because people found it hard to accept me as normal. Some people you run into, no matter how hard you try to convince them, never treat you as a real person. They see you as this weird thing. When I would go to buy my bakery goods for example, the girl in the store would break out in a rash every time I walked in. I've been there a million times and it's only recently that she has stopped breaking out in a rash when she sees me!

MD: *There has been a lot of talk recently about the dearth of good roles for women in Hollywood. Do you find that the scripts sent to you are not terribly interesting?*

AM: They are horrible and when you find one that's really good, it just makes you so happy. This is a very intense subject for me. I think in general the way women are portrayed limits them completely. This whole emphasis now on the fragile little waif is so frustrating because I am unhappy with my size and I'm skinny! When I'm in Montana I feel fine and thin. Whenever I go to Hollywood I feel fat. Sharon Stone made it with a very sexual character but that is not what women are about. That is a man's sexual fantasy of what women are about.

MD: *Is that very frustrating for you as an actress, particularly when you read that Sharon Stone is now regarded as one of the few actresses who can automatically close a multi-million-dollar deal in Hollywood?*

AM: It is frustrating as an actress but more so as a woman, because it makes me unhappy in my personal life. The people that I find really beautiful are not emaciated, sexual, hot-to-trot, crotch-showing women. That is not the type of woman I want to be with. Women are wonderful characters and this is not shown in many films. That is sad. Sharon Stone is laughing all the way to the bank. Does that mean I have to behave like her if I want to go to the bank myself? It is completely depressing.

MD: *Both yourself and Jodie Foster have spoken out strongly on this recent trend in Hollywood and both of you have made successful films this year. Do you think this will help restore the image of women?*

AM: I must have a conversation with her! It's just that I like characters like the girl in *An Angel at My Table*; that was a wonderful, complex, interesting woman. That's the type of woman I would like to be with. Particularly the one character in *Enchanted April*, not Miranda Richardson, the other one...

MD: *... Josie Lawrence?*

AM: Yes. Now that's the kind of woman I would like to be around and also the type of woman that I would like to portray – a complex, interesting woman.

MD: *You mentioned your frustration at the tendency to cast five-foot-three actresses in waif roles. It must have been nice for you to play opposite six-foot-four Liam Neeson in* Ruby Cairo...

AM: Even on that one, the guy was telling me to lose weight! But the height thing with Liam was wonderful and it made me feel thin!

MD: *You spend a lot of time in interviews talking about your children. They are obviously the most important thing in your life...*

AM: I know. I probably should spend my time talking about my character and my motivation. But I do think that my career is helped by my being a mother. What happens to me in life helps me develop characters and gives me something to draw from. I don't think I could portray a mother, for example, if I didn't have children of my own. And my family are all-important to me.

MD: *Is that why you live in Montana, away from the LA rat-race?*

AM: I couldn't live in LA, the people there are too driven and it would drive me absolutely out of my mind. I love living in the country and even though I used to live outside New York, it was a great change going to the country. I never believe anything anybody in LA tells me. They are totally full of baloney. They just lie! They'll say anything to you just to get your attention. In New York, they may be blunt but at least you know the truth. I'd rather people were frank and said "I really cannot see you in this role" instead of bullshitting me and wasting my time.

MD: *From what has been written about you it would appear that you didn't have such a happy childhood. Is that why you place so much emphasis on your own family?*

AM: Well, my mother was an alcoholic so, even though she was wonderful and I had a marvellous relationship with her, I couldn't say she was very strong. But she was also kind of trapped in society. Back then it was a stigma to be an alcoholic and there wasn't the emphasis on AA that there is today. We all try to imitate our parents but I try not to make the same mistakes. If I ever see myself doing something that they did I think, "Oh no!" I would never have an argument in front of my children. If I was arguing with my husband, my children would never hear it.

MD: *Do you feel bitter about your upbringing now?*

AM: Bitter? No, I'm not bitter. I'm sad and it hurts sometimes. My mother died when I was 23 and there were so many things I didn't discuss with her. My situation with my father was also difficult because he remarried and was gone. I think my father and stepmother are getting sick of me. I use my interviews as a form of analysis! Where else would you get the opportunity to sit around and talk about this stuff?

POSTSCRIPT

At the time of the interview, Andie MacDowell was working on Short Cuts *for Robert Altman, which she would go on to describe as one of her finest movies. The actress subsequently topped the US and UK charts simultaneously with* Bad Girls *and* Four Weddings and a Funeral, *respectively. The latter film proved a huge money-maker, since MacDowell accepted a lower rate than usual for the film, but availed of a profit share from the world-wide smash hit.*

MOVIEGUIDE'S 10 FAVOURITE FILMS OF ALL TIME, FROM 100 YEARS OF CINEMA

1   *La Grande Illusion* (Jean Renoir, 1937)
Beautifully realised anti-war statement which also examines the rigidity of the social class structure.

2   *Duck Soup* (Leo McCarey, 1933)
The Marxes' finest hour: no harps, no pianos, just mayhem.

3   *L'Atalante* (Jean Vigo, 1934)
Vigo's floating *meisterwerk* is a paean to romance and aspiration.

4 *Manhattan* [Woody Allen, 1979]
Woody's New York valentine is witty, incisive and definitely not a candidate for The Academy of the Over-rated.

5 *The Godfather Part II* [Francis Ford Coppola, 1974]
Sprawling family saga which exceeds its magnificent predecessor by virtue of its enlarged scope and the presence of one Robert DeNiro.

6 *Singin' in the Rain* [Stanley Donen, 1952]
The musical *du jour*, without which no desert island journey is complete.

7 *The Long Day Closes* [Terence Davies, 1989]
The poet of modern cinema decorates the screen with an array of evocative visual and audio images.

8 *Tokyo Story* [Yasujiro Ozu, 1953]
Almost painful to watch, Ozu's detailed study focuses on the lines that are drawn between familial duty, obligation and love.

9 *The Adventures of Robin Hood* [Michael Curtiz, 1938]
In like Flynn. Despite the green tights, Curtiz's Technicolor swashbuckler marked the Tasmanian devil out from the pack. 'Are you with me, men?'

10 *Paths of Glory* [Stanley Kubrick, 1957]
Kubrick's travelling camera dives among the WWI trenches to create cinema's second-most powerful anti-war statement. Kirk Douglas has seldom been better; George MacCready has seldom been badder.

TAKE
TEN
DAMON ALBARN

The section in which various personalities have been given three minutes to answer ten revealing questions about their cinema-going habits. Next up is Damon Albarn, Chelsea fan and lead singer of hip, post–modern popsters Blur.

1   *If you were to be stranded on a desert island with nothing but a VCR and three films, what titles would you choose?*

Meantime (Mike Leigh; 1983, US), *Women on the Verge...* (Pedro Almodovar; 1988, Sp.) and *The Godfather Part II* (Coppola; 1974, US)

2   *What was the most recent film you saw and how would you rate it out of ten?*

Golden Balls. Eight out of ten.

3   *When was the last time you cried at the movies?*

I cried out of sheer frustration at *Four Weddings and a Funeral.* I find Hugh Grant nauseating.

The director and cast of "Women on the Verge of a Nervous Breakdown"

4 *Who was your first movie star pin-up?*

Michael Caine as *Alfie*.

5 *Who is the actor or actress who most makes you want to throw your popcorn at the screen in disgust?*

Winona Ryder, a dreadful actress.

6 *How many of The Magnificent Seven can you name?*

Morrissey, Ray Davis, Johnny Marr, Paul Weller, Johnny Rotten, John Lennon and Paul Jones.

7 *What is your attitude to sub-titles?*

I like 'em.

8 *Who is the finest actor you have ever seen?*

In a provincial way, it would be Gary Oldman, Tim Roth or Phil Daniels.

9 *If Hollywood were planning to film the story of your life, who would you like to see in the title role?*

I'd find that very distressing. I'd prefer Pinewood Studios to do it, but I wouldn't want that degree of immortality, anyway. You get remembered for the wrong things if Hollywood gets its hands on your life. It's all far too egocentric.

10 *And what would it be called?*

I Don't Wanna Do it!

KING LEER

Groucho Marx

To say that certain performers were "before their time" has become such a cliché that it scarcely has any meaning any more. In the case of the Marx Brothers, however, it is entirely true. Their irreverent humour is as relevant today as it was in 1929 when Groucho, Chico and Harpo (you're on your own, Zeppo) arrived in Hollywood, fresh from conquering vaudeville and Broadway, and took the town by storm. Chico was the quasi-Italian and Harpo the silent clown but Groucho, with the sloping walk, greasepaint moustache and permanent cigar, was the main man. His timing and delivery of brilliantly written barbs single-handedly ensured that the Marxes would never be categorised with the pie-in-the-face, slapstick humour which was prevalent when they began their screen career.

Whether, er, wooing Margaret Dumont or engaged in illogical badinage with Chico, Groucho was always hilarious, and throughout his screen career he provided an array of immortal characters. These included Rufus T. Firefly ("Do you love me? Did he leave you any money? Answer the second

question first"); Dr Hugo Z. Hackenbush ("Either he's dead or my watch has stopped"); Professor Quincy Adams Wagstaff ("You've got the brain of a four-year-old child, and I bet he was glad to get rid of it") and Captain Geoffrey Spaulding ("You're the most beautiful woman I've ever seen. Which doesn't say much for you").

Though most of these classic lines were originated by some of the greatest writers in the business, including George S. Kaufman, Morrie Ryskind, S.J. Perelman and Nat Perrin, there is no doubt that Groucho's delivery was the key. He would use this skill in later years when making his mark on the popular television show *You Bet Your*

Life. But it wasn't until the Seventies, when the Marxes became cult heroes with the likes of Woody Allen and Dick Cavett, that his reputation was secured. Anyone who doubts Groucho Marx's place in the pantheon of screen greats need only sit through the dross that passes itself off as Hollywood comedy today and compare it to anything produced by the Marx Brothers.

THE PICK OF GROUCHO

Duck Soup (1933)

The Marxes' finest hour, with Groucho as Fredonia ruler Rufus T. Firefly dividing his time between wooing Mrs Rittenhouse ("Remember, men. We're fighting for this woman's honour. Which is probably more than she ever did") and starting a war with neighbouring Sylvania ("I've already paid a month's rent on the battlefield"). Panned at the time, today *Duck Soup* is considered a satiric masterpiece.

A Night at the Opera (1935)

When Irving Thalberg took the Marxes to MGM he decided to set them up in a lavish production and balance the zaniness of their Paramount features with a strong plot and good musical interludes. *Night at the Opera* was the result with Groucho in top form as opera guru Otis B. Driftwood. This is the one with the famous stateroom sequence ("Is my Aunt Minnie in here?") and the one where Chico is giving a speech while pretending to be a famous Russian aviator ("Talk fast, I see a man in the crowd with a rope").

A Day at the Races (1937)

After *Night at the Opera* proved the Marxes' biggest success, Thalberg kept the formula going in *A Day at the Races*. Groucho played horse doctor Hugo Z. Hackenbush employed at a sanatorium ("You've nothing to worry about. The last person I gave one of those to won the Kentucky Derby") run by Maureen O'Sullivan. Plenty of great scenes including the rare sight of Chico putting one over on Groucho with his 'tootsie-frootsie ice cream' routine, and the hilarious medical examination sequence ("Well, I must say I've seen quicker examinations"/ "Maybe, but you'll never see a slippier one").

REEL 6

THIS BOY'S LIFE

Gabriel Byrne has long been one of our most successful actors on stage, screen and television. His curriculum vitae is well known: suffice it to mention Drimnagh, UCD, teaching, The Project, The Riordans, Bracken, Excalibur, Miller's Crossing and Into the West. Now separated from his wife Ellen Barkin, with whom he has two children, Jack and Romy, when we spoke 45–year–old Gabriel had recently published a collection of autobiographical reminisces, Pictures in My Head.

Michael Doherty:

What was the genesis of
Pictures in My Head?

Gabriel Byrne:

It was really a combination
of a few things. I used to go
out with Áine O'Connor,
who worked in RTE a long
time ago, and she was always
on at me to do things. She
kept saying, "You should
write that down". I used to
do essays at school in return
for maths problems and that
got me interested in the
whole idea of writing.

MD: *Why did you decide to write it at
this stage in your life and career?*

GB: It was an attempt to find
something out about myself.
I think writing is a magical,
mysterious process and the
physical act of writing
changes your perception of
things. I wanted it to be
some sort of record for my
kids. I felt that if I wrote it
honestly enough, then in
years to come they would
know something of the kind
of person I was.

MD: *There is a very strong father/son
connection running through the
book which reaches its apotheosis
when you compare the day your
son Jack was born to a day you
spent in Kildare with your
father...*

GB: That was probably the most
important part of it for me.
I see a connection between
my son and my father and
his place in the whole
scheme of things. But it's
also to see my own place
between father and son
because I am now a father. I
always thought of myself as
a son and now I'm a father.
That relationship for a lot of
men is a very complex one
because it is tied up with so
many layers of emotion,
feeling and complexity. I
really was standing there in
the hotel room that night
looking at this thing in the
crib and saying, "What is

this? What am I now?" I had this picture in my head of me strolling down the road with my father and I realised, I am now him. I have become my own father.

MD: *Do you feel that this is a peculiarly Irish thing, or a feeling which comes to every man at some stage in his life?*

GB: It is something peculiar to Ireland. I remember going through a stage reading a lot of Irish literature and there was very little written about the mother/son relationship but an awful lot about the father/son relationship. There is a beautiful story by Donncha Ó Ceilleachair called "Mac an Chait" about a father and son working together on a bog. Liam O'Flaherty has some beautiful stories such as "An Buille" and there's Frank O'Connor's "My Oedipus Complex". It could be that Irish men express themselves in print because they are slow to express themselves in person, in case they look weak. Where that notion

came from, I don't know.

MD: *Do you find this fear of expression in Los Angeles?*

GB: No, I certainly don't find it in America. One of the reasons that I love living in LA is that I am validated every day for the kind of person I am. I don't mean that people remark, "There's yer man from that movie" or whatever, but people would say, "That's an interesting idea" or "That's nice of you to say that". They are forthcoming about compliments and it is no big deal to them. An Irish person might say something complimentary if they had twelve pints in them!

MD: *Do you find it easy to write?*

GB: Not really, but then I didn't sit down with a preconceived notion of writing, to make it chronological or whatever. I decided to write about whatever came up. For example, one incident that I remember was going to school with this nun who told us these incredible stories about Irish nationalism and her brother who had been killed by the Black and Tans. I was six at the time and I recall this incredible story of the guy in a white shirt which was turning red with his blood.

MD: *I remember that story. Do you think it was true or just something she told every class?*

GB: The strange thing is, this woman was the sister of a famous GAA player from the Twenties. Whether it really happened, I don't know, but she told it with amazing conviction.

MD: *What do you remember most about those early schooldays?*

GB: I remember the Dickensian approach to discipline. The nuns taught with fear, they didn't teach with praise and approval. For a long time, I was very bitter about that because I realised that an awful lot of my life was based on fear and, to a great extent, shame. I think I was taught that at school level but it's gone now. The difference between me going to school for the first time in that bus on a wet Monday morning in Dublin, and bringing my son to school in LA, was like millions of light years. I said to Jack, "C'mon, we'll get our photo taken", and he said, "No, Dad, I don't want to have my photo taken", and I thought that was great! I never would have had that control.

MD: *Did you have any worries when Jack was going to school that he would be singled out as Gabriel Byrne's son?*

GB: Thank God, but it's one of my least fears. He goes to a school where his best friend has two mothers. They are a gay couple who have adopted this child. Here is this gay woman in LA telling me, "I sometimes worry when he gets to 13, what the kids will say to him", and I tell her, "You know, if you love this child, and your partner loves this child, then he is going to start off with a great advantage in life, whatever he does." That's what I like about living in

LA. You are forced to confront things that are different from your natural old Irish beliefs. At first you say, "God, two mothers!" but after you have talked to them for a few minutes, you realise they love this kid and the kid loves them, and why can't the world be made up of all kinds of different forms of love?

MD: *There is great attention to detail in your book, recalling Trigger bars and Marietta biscuits and so forth. Did you keep a diary or are those ingrained memories?*

GB: I never kept a diary though I often wish I did. But the subconscious is an amazing thing, as I'm sure you've found yourself when you are writing. I mean, I'm sitting in LA, but I can see a Trigger bar. I can see the blue paper and the ridges all along it and I can taste it. And I remember cream pies, marshmallow mice and Peggy's Leg. As a child I had a great sense of smell and colour. Even now I can see a colour and it can suddenly remind me of a guy's pencil in the class when I was six years old.

MD: *There is a great deal about your father in the book and you mention that he was always saying you'd be a great scholar one day. What would he have made of your autobiography?*

GB: That's a great question, what would he have made of it. My father never finished a sentence, you know. He would say something like "Ah... now" and nod his head sideways. When you put that on the page it means nothing but I know what he meant by it. If I gave him the book, he would probably say, "Be the hokey, man." He wouldn't say, "I thought your attention to detail was incredible and I thought some of the characters were extremely well delineated."

MD: *What type of man was he?*

GB: My father was a man who came from a rural background, worked in Guinness's, read the paper at night, and that was that. I never saw my father with a book. He took us to the movies once. It was *The Bridge on the River Kwai* and the usher had to come along after two minutes and wake him up because he was snoring! And he had been talking about this trip for weeks.

MD: *How did he react to your own plays or films?*

GB: He came to see me in a play, one of the first I was ever in, *Borstal Boy* at the Gaiety. I said to him afterwards, "How did you like it?" And he said, "Ah janey... well now..." And he had fallen asleep! I know, because I was on stage and I saw him, and his head was bobbing back and forth!

MD: *Appearing in* The Riordans *must have been a different matter...*

GB: Oh yes, his biggest kick was seeing me in *The Riordans*. I don't think I could ever have got a bigger kick myself. I grew up with that programme and it really was a dream come true to be on

it. My father couldn't believe watching me on television and seeing me at the same time sitting on the couch beside him.

MD: *Was that an exciting time in your own life?*

GB: Nothing has ever surpassed that in terms of excitement. The excitement of that in 1978 was unbelievable. People were coming up to me in the street and saying things like, "Jaysus, that Benjy will put manners on ya, ya boy ya." You're into the whole area of people saying, "Are you who I think you are?"

MD: *When I interviewed the Coen Brothers recently, they mentioned that you had bullied them into making the main character of* Miller's Crossing *an Irishman, and what set out to be a Jewish gangster ended up as Tom Regan. Any truth in that?*

GB: Yeah. I read that piece. I think you mostly dwelt on *Barton Fink*. It's true, I did bully them into making Tom Regan an Irishman! Actually, after we had finished filming,

Brosnan: shaken, not stirred

One of the all–time greats, "Paths of Glory"

Oscar glory for Holly Hunter

Andie McDowell in "Four Weddings and a Funeral"

Arnold Schwarzenegger in "Last Action Hero"

Sandra Bullock in "Speed"

Uma Thurman in "Pulp Fiction"

The two faces of Daniel Day–Lewis: "In the Name of the Father" and "The Age of Innocence"

On the set of "In the Name of the Father" with Jim Sheridan

Tom Hanks in "Forrest Gump" (above) and in "Apollo 13" (below)

Johnny Depp in "Edward Scissorhands" (above) and "Don Juan de Marcos" (below)

I told the Coens to look me up if they were ever in Dublin. One Sunday, and it was the day of an All-Ireland final, I received a call from Joel Coen to say that he was in O'Connell Street. I took them to a quiet guest house in Ballsbridge, told them to settle in, and I would collect them before going to a play that night. When I arrived, I was greeted by a bizarre sight: Joel and Ethan Coen sitting on a sofa with the family of the house, eating a meat and spuds dinner, and happily watching *Glenroe!*

MD: *You mentioned that you had learnt a lot about yourself through writing your autobiography. Did this act as a catharsis for you while you and Ellen were going through the break-up?*

GB: Not really. I had to deal with all that stuff head-on because you can't get away from it. I had to deal with it in what I thought was a realistic way. The book actually became a bit of a millstone because I had to deal with that at the same time. It wasn't any kind of release in me, it was never anything like that. I only ever found a release when I confronted the reality of the pain that I was going through in the split-up of my relationship. The only way around pain is through it; I've discovered that.

MD: *Are you through it now?*

GB: Yes, I have to say that I am.

MD: *And stronger as a result?*

GB: I would say much stronger. I mean, I think I had my own kind of male menopause through my twenties. I had a really unhappy twenties, and my thirties weren't particularly happy, either. But when I reached about 38 or 39, I began to suddenly think, "I know what this is all about." I've been happy for the past five years. Even with the break-up, during which I fell into a slough of despondency. But I'm happy now and I'm happy that I can say that. I remember telling a friend of mine in LA that I was waiting for the axe to fall, and he said, "That's an Irish thing, get rid of that, it doesn't have to fall." I'm going around content and I feel that I'm entitled and deserve to be content. I know what my weak points are.

MD: *Such as?*

GB: Well, I tend to be introverted, I tend to be isolated, I tend to be a loner who can cut himself off from people. Now I'm beginning to open myself out. The book is a way of saying, "I'm not afraid to admit any more that I'm an actor, that I'm a writer."

MD: *One passage in the opening section of the book simply says, "In 1993 my marriage broke up." Was that easy for you to write?*

GB: It wasn't easy but it was something I had to do in the same way I want to remember moments like the time our son was born and Ellen asked me what I was thinking and I told her my thoughts as we sat in that room together. I don't want to remember the moment when we said, "Look, this isn't working any more", and went in opposite directions.

POSTSCRIPT

After we had finished the interview, which was conducted in a Dublin hotel lounge, Gabriel demonstrated that his claim to have a great sense of recall from the past was not an idle one. One women who had been keeping a close eye on him (and there were many in the vicinity that day) from a nearby table approached the actor after the interview and introduced herself as someone whose family used to live near his mother's house, adding the usual proviso that he probably wouldn't remember. Not only could he remember the house, he remembered each of the family members, their nicknames and a host of little incidents. She left the hotel, like I did, mightily impressed with Gabriel Byrne.

MOVIEGUIDE'S 10 FAVOURITE MOVIE DID-YOU-KNOWS?

1 It has been calculated that the phrase "Let's get out of here" occurs in 84 per cent of all Hollywood movies.

2 Cary Grant was 55 when he appeared in Hitchcock's *North by Northwest* (1959). Jessie Royce Landis played his mother in the film. She was 54.

3 Stewart Granger's real name was James Stewart; Michael Keaton's real name is Michael Douglas, and Michael Douglas's real name is Stewart Granger. OK, maybe not (but the first two are true enough).

4 The "blood" used by Alfred Hitchcock in the infamous shower sequence from *Psycho* (1960) was, in fact, chocolate sauce.

5 While Robert DeNiro was preparing to play middleweight champ Jake La Motta in *Raging Bull* (1980) he fought three professional bouts under the name Young Jake, winning two.

6 John Ford's classic *The Grapes of Wrath* (1940) was banned in Russia because it showed a poverty-stricken family who could still afford a car.

7 The f-word was used in Martin Scorsese's *GoodFellas* 246 times (mostly by Joe Pesci, one suspects).

8 *Some Like it Hot* (1959) was originally conceived as a vehicle for Bob Hope and Danny Kaye.

9 The first Academy Awards ceremony in 1929 lasted four minutes and 22 seconds. (Meanwhile, Greer Garson's Best Actress acceptance speech for *Mrs Miniver* in 1942 lasted over an hour.)

10 At the height of her (and their) popularity, Cyd Charisse's legs were insured for $10 million.

ALL ABOUT BETTE

Bette Davis

The over-ripe heroine, the Queen Bitch, the mistress of *Grand Guignol*. Only one actress could take on each of these personalities in film roles and redefine the category: Bette Davis. The Queen of Warners did not have the benefit of what were described as conventional movie star looks ("I was the first star who ever came out of the water looking wet," she herself declared), but few could match her acting range. And few, too, could escape her caustic tongue.

When she began to establish herself in Hollywood (she had already won two Oscars by 1937), she fought tooth and nail with Jack Warner for better roles. The studio reacted by suspending her but Davis earned much respect for taking a stand, and her fight over contracts was

eventually won by her friend, Olivia De Havilland. Davis's CV is littered with great moments: receiving two lit cigarettes from Paul Henreid in *Now Voyager* (1942); giving Miriam Hopkins a good shaking in *Old Acquaintance* (1943); serving Joan Crawford a cooked rat in *Whatever Happened to Baby Jane?* (1962), and delivering bilious comments with gay abandon in *All About Eve* (1950): "Fasten your seat-belts. It's going to be a bumpy night!"

On the bumpy night she received the American Film Institute Award from her peers, Davis reminded the audience of her own favourite line from all her movies. The film was *Cabin in the Cotton* (1932), the recipient was Richard Barthelmess, and the line was pure Bette: "I'd love to kiss yah, but I just washed mah hair."

THE PICK OF BETTE

All About Eve (1950)
Davis's finest hour and a film script (by writer/director Joseph Mankiewicz) which seemed to be dipped in acid. Originally intended for Claudette Colbert, the central role of ageing actress Margo Channing is tailor-made for Davis, who relishes the opportunity to cross tongues with waspish critic George Sanders and too-good-to-be-true acolyte Anne Baxter. "Remind me to tell you about the time I looked into the heart of an artichoke."

Whatever Happened to Baby Jane? (1962)
Robert Aldrich's supreme slice of *Grand Guignol* made all the headlines for the undisguised contempt that existed between the two leading ladies, Davis and Joan Crawford. Stories circulated about the venom of the screen slaps delivered by Davis to her wheelchair-bound sister; while Crawford was said to have got her own back by filling her skirt with lead weights in a scene where Davis has to drag Crawford along the floor. All this and cooked rats, too.

Jezebel (1938)
The film which Davis considered a sop for not getting to play Scarlett O'Hara is another highlight in the actress's canon. Davis relished the role of a spoilt Southern belle, and provided a great moment by arriving at an important ball in that striking red dress (pity that the film was not shot in colour).

REEL 7

LUNCH WITH SIGOURNEY

12.59pm. Sixty seconds ahead of the appointed luncheon tryst with Sigourney Weaver and I am tapping, gingerly, on the door of her hotel room. One of Ms Weaver's assistants invites me to enter the inner sanctum before escorting me to a nearby table. The hotel room is vast and luxurious, befitting the status of one of Tinseltown's finest actresses. On the far side of the room, the star of Working Girl, Gorillas in the Mist *and the* Alien *trilogy is sitting on the edge of her bed, her personal assistant applying the finishing touches to her make–up.*

Satisfied, the actress rises and proceeds to greet me with a disarming smile and a firm handshake. Tall, very tall, and stylishly dressed (befitting a Yale graduate who culled her name from an F. Scott Fitzgerald novel), Susan Weaver is a joy to interview: talkative, amusing and generous with her time — making her something of a rara avis *among her peers. Today she is here to talk about her role in Ivan Reitman's* Dave, *in which she plays the First Lady to Kevin Kline's President.*

Michael Doherty:

> *What attracted you to the idea of playing the First Lady in your latest film,* Dave*?*

Sigourney Weaver:

> I think I liked it because it is a real vacation from reality. I don't see the film as a political satire; I see it as a satire on the American Dream which says that anyone can grow up and become President. It is a sentimental view which says that, with things in a mess, anybody can walk off the streets and into the White House to do a better job balancing the budget with a pen and paper! We hope that this could be true and I think it is very cathartic for Americans to laugh at these things because it has been a difficult and confusing time politically at home.

MD: *It's a very Capra–esque film. One can imagine Cary Grant and Jean Arthur in the lead roles...*

SW: Yes, I believe it is. It's like an old-fashioned, stylish, romantic movie. Like Capra, certainly, but hipper!

MD: *When the film was written, Bush was President. By the time it was released, Clinton was in the Oval Office. Did that make a significant difference to how the film was received?*

SW: There was always a big argument as to whether it would do better if Bush were still in the White House. Some were saying that it's because Clinton is President that people can come and laugh about politics, but I don't think it would make much difference. In some ways it would be funnier if Bush were still there because Kevin and I thought we were playing Republicans!

MD: *Was that a conscious* Aliens *reference in* Dave *where Kevin Kline is wearing the mechanical gear that you wore as Ripley?*

SW: I think they just showed up at the factory and that's what the gear was like. Interesting that you thought that, though. I'll mention it to Ivan Reitman: Hey Ivan, unconscious homage!

MD: *Most people would see Sigourney Weaver in the forefront of the campaign for equality for women in Hollywood, particularly after the protest you generated over your fee for* Alien[3]. *Do you see yourself in that light?*

SW: I don't think I'm a crusader but I'm certainly a realist. There may be more men's roles out there but many of them are not that interesting, either. As actors, because this is what we do, we are all trying to criticise constructively so that more interesting movies are made and more chances taken. I think that's why Jodie Foster started her own production company. It's certainly why I

did. I don't really think I am at the forefront of anything in Hollywood, though, because I live in New York, and I try not to think of Hollywood too much.

MD: *Why not?*

SW: Because I think that people in Hollywood have a great respect for actors but also a great suspicion of them. You know, we are these people who work with our emotions and might suddenly fly off into a frenzy! When I go to Hollywood, the producers are respectful but they look at me as if I am some sort of creature!

MD: *Is your attitude towards Hollywood tempered by the fact that you come from a theatrical background and didn't learn your craft on-screen?*

SW: Probably, and also because I am married to a theatre director who would shrivel up and die if we moved to Hollywood! As a person, I find that LA is a wonderful reverie in that you can drive around and not see anything upsetting. But I actually feel safer in New York because I know what the reality is and I can see everything going on around me. I don't want to wake up in two years time and realise, "Oh the world is in a terrible mess." I'd rather live where it is happening so I know what is going on.

MD: *In the wake of Ripley, we have seen many actresses, including Bridget Fonda and Rene Russo, taking the lead in action movies. Is this just a fad or are women going to be taken seriously in what has almost exclusively become a boy's club in Hollywood?*

SW: I have taken ten years to make sure that women are taken seriously as an action figure. There are great suspense stories out there and I can see no reason why women shouldn't play the pivotal roles. Women are playing these parts in real life, so there is no reason why films shouldn't mirror reality.

MD: *You have mentioned that you are planning to cut down on your acting schedule to spend more time with your daughter, Charlotte. What are your concerns for her?*

SW: I am concerned with finding the right school for her. There are a lot of good schools but mostly they are single-sex. We are happy in Manhattan but we would certainly move if there was a perfect school to be found. I worry about things. Sometimes in New York you say, "Oh gosh, we are living in a hard city. " But yet, when I drive back and see the skyline, I am thrilled to be there.

MD: *Have you any ambitions to get behind the camera?*

SW: I know there are great directors that I would like to work with, the likes of Coppola and Scorsese, for example, but some day I would like to do something very humble myself. It will be interesting because I like actors and I respect what they do. I couldn't be a director like the big guys, but I would like to direct something, some day.

MD: *Which of your own films do you look back on with most fondness?*

SW: I think that of all the films I've made, *The Year of Living Dangerously* holds up the best because it is about something so much bigger than the people in it. I really find that attractive about the film. It's hard to find that nowadays. Hollywood seems to make movies which are just about people and little else. I am still amazed, also, by working with the gorillas and the problems that Dian faced.

MD: *Do you feel underpaid in Hollywood compared with your male counterparts?*

SW: I feel well paid compared with my husband who gets absolutely nothing for working in the theatre! I don't really care how much Arnold gets: if he gets it, fine. People like Julia Roberts and Sharon Stone, the new group, should gouge them and take all the money they can. But I don't worry about how much these guys get. What do they do with all that money? It's such an unreal amount and it doesn't mean anything to me. I only really thought about it for *Alien³* because what they were offering me was so insulting, just galling. And I'm glad that I made such a huge stink about it!

POSTSCRIPT

Following Dave, *Sigourney Weaver cut back on her film schedule. She returned with a bang in Roman Polanski's screen adaptation of Ariel Dorfman's* Death and the Maiden, *delivering the finest performance of her career. The fact that she wasn't even nominated for an Oscar is one of the greatest travesties in recent Oscar history. Her latest film is the thriller* Copycat, *co-starring Holly Hunter.*

MOVIEGUIDE'S 20 MOVIE MIGHT-HAVE-BEENS

There are many classic roles which have been created by actors who were not the original choice. For reasons of health, commitments, dismissal, or the inability to recognise a good part when they saw it, actors have often passed up a great opportunity. Consider the following:

• Oscar winner ° Oscar nominee

STAR	FILM	ORIGINAL CHOICE
Clint Eastwood	*Dirty Harry* (1971)	Frank Sinatra
John Travolta°	*Pulp Fiction* (1994)	Michael Madsen
Harrison Ford	*Raiders of the Lost Ark* (1981)	Tom Selleck
Charlton Heston•	*Ben–Hur* (1959)	Cesare Danova
Martin Sheen	*Apocalypse Now* (1979)	Harvey Keitel
Bette Davis°	*All About Eve* (1950)	Claudette Colbert
Kathleen Turner	*Body Heat* (1982)	Sigourney Weaver
Fred MacMurray	*Double Indemnity* (1944)	Alan Ladd
Judy Garland	*The Wizard of Oz* (1939)	Shirley Temple
Frank Sinatra•	*From Here To Eternity* (1953)	Eli Wallach
Faye Dunaway°	*Chinatown* (1974)	Ali McGraw
Dustin Hoffman°	*The Graduate* (1967)	Robert Redford
Michelle Pfeiffer	*Batman Returns* (1992)	Annette Bening
Humphry Bogart• / Kate Hepburn°	*The African Queen* (1951)	David Niven / Bette Davis

STAR	FILM	ORIGINAL CHOICE
Humphrey Bogart° / Ingrid Bergman	*Casablanca* (1942)	Michele Morgan / Dennis Morgan
Mia Farrow	*Rosemary's Baby* (1968)	Jane Fonda
Humphrey Bogart	*The Maltese Falcon* (1941)	George Raft
William Holden / Gloria Swanson°	*Sunset Boulevard* (1950)	Montgomery Clift / Mae West
Errol Flynn	*The Adventures of Robin Hood* (1938)	James Cagney
Peter O'Toole°	*Lawrence of Arabia* (1962)	Albert Finney

Could you imagine anybody else?

TAKE
TEN
QUENTIN TARANTINO

The section in which various personalities are given three minutes to answer ten revealing questions about their cinema-going habits. Next up is writer-director Quentin Tarantino, who burst onto the scene with his debut feature, Reservoir Dogs, *and consolidated his position as the hottest property in Hollywood by taking both the Palme D'Or at Cannes and an Oscar for his second feature,* Pulp Fiction.

1 *If you were to be stranded on a desert island with nothing but a VCR and three films, what titles would you choose?*

Taxi Driver (Scorsese; 1976, US), *Rio Bravo* (Hawks; 1959, US) and *His Girl Friday* (Hawks; 1940, US)

2 *What was the most recent film you saw and how would you rate it out of ten?*

The last film I saw was Alexandre Rockwell's *Somebody To Love,* with Harvey Keitel and Rosie Perez. I loved it and I'd give it an eight.

3 *When was the last time you cried at the movies?*

That's an unfair question for me because I am a sucker! Actually, I cried at a film I saw at the Venice Film Festival, Peter Jackson's *Heavenly Creatures.*

4 *Who is the finest actor or actress you have ever seen?*

I don't know about finest. I just have, like, favourites. I don't have one favourite actor or actress; I have, like, collections of favourites. For a long period, Harvey Keitel was a big favourite of mine, even before I met him. And another hero was Michael Parkes, who appeared in some television series in the Sixties.

5 *Who is the actor or actress who most makes you want to throw your popcorn at the screen in disgust?*

I don't think I had better answer that!

6   *What is your attitude to sub-titles?*

I love sub-titles and I much prefer them to dubbing.

7   *How many of the 12 Angry Men can you name?*

Actually, I've never seen *12 Angry Men*, though I loved the play. But just from knowledge, there's Henry Fonda, Jack Klugman, E.G. Marshall, Jack Warden, that guy, Kerensky or Kersky, I could never pronounce his name. Those are the names off the top of my head but I can name all The Magnificent Seven, even Brad Dexter. And I can name all those who escaped in *The Great Escape*.

8   *How are you on the Dirty Dozen?*

OK, let's see. Lee Marvin, Charles Bronson, Telly Savalas, John Cassavetes, Jim Brown, Trini Lopez, Donald Sutherland, that guy who became a director, Robert Cooper, Clint Walker. Was Richard Jaeckel one? It's always hard to say. Let's consider him one for the purposes of this study!

9   *If Hollywood were planning to film the story of your life, who would you like to see in the title role?*

Tom Cruise! Actually Oliver Stone is going to make a story about my life. No, seriously, I'd say Johnny Depp.

10   *And what would it be called?*

I don't know but if Oliver Stone made it, he would probably cast Val Kilmer as me and it would probably be called *QT!*

Dog eat Dog for Steve and Harvey

TRIBUTE TO A BAD MAN

James Cagney

Whether he was pushing a grapefruit into Mae Murray's face, laughing maniacally atop a gas tank or slapping any number of guys and dolls, James Francis Cagney was the quintessential tough guy. Raised on the East Side of New York, Cagney incorporated a lot of the hard nuts he saw growing up into his characters, notably Rocky 'whaddya hear, whaddya say' Sullivan in *Angels With Dirty Faces* (1938).

Yet of all the classic screen gangsters – Bogart, Robinson, Raft – Cagney was the least comfortable in the role. He was first and foremost a hoofer, a Columbia-educated performer who was raised on the vaudeville stage, where he made his debut as a female impersonator.

Cagney's magnificent, Oscar-winning performance in the musical *Yankee Doodle Dandy* thus came as no surprise to those who knew him in

the early days of his career.

But it was the tough guy who the public lined up to see. And Cagney was the best. "Never settle back on your heels and never relax," was his motto and in film after film, he was true to his word. Cagney was an unexploded bomb and one never quite knew when the hair trigger would go off. "Say, you're a snappy lookin' dame," was about as romantic as he got with Ann Sheridan, and

that suited his public fine.

Yet Cagney was more than just a screen heavy. His later films, notably, *The Man of a Thousand Faces*, *Mr Roberts*, *Love Me or Leave Me* and *One, Two, Three,* demonstrated an actor at the height of his talents. He never said, 'All right, you guys', and he never said, 'You dirty rat!'; that was a fallacy. But James Cagney was a superb actor, and that's the truth, see.

THE PICK OF CAGNEY

The Public Enemy (1931)

Originally cast as the milder of two street kids in this early Warners gangster pic, Cagney exchanged hats with Eddie Woods and became Tom Powers. The rest is grapefruits, hard-boiled dialogue ("I wish you was a wishing well so I could tie a bucket to you and sink you") and history. A star was born.

White Heat (1949)

After a few years away from the Warners fold, Cagney returned with a bang as Cody Jarrett, the

sniggering psychopath who wreaks havoc before going out in a blaze of glory: "Made it, ma, top of the world!"

Love Me or Leave Me (1955)

Not one of the more famous Cagney vehicles but neither he nor co-star Doris Day have ever been better. In this biopic of torch singer Ruth Etting, Cagney is outstanding as Marty the Gimp Snyder, the two-bit crook guiding her fortunes whose interest in the star is far from philanthrophic.

Cagney with Sylvia Sidney in "Blood on the Sun" (1945)

JOHNNY
FRIENDLY

Johnny Depp is not your average Hollywood heart-throb. He eschews the celebrity scene and avoids films which play solely on his dark, Cherokee looks. With the possible exception of Edward Scissorhands *and the television series,* 21 Jump Street *Depp has become as famous for his (now ended) liaison with actress Winona Ryder as for his acting.*

Born in Owensboro, Kentucky in 1963, Depp grew up in Florida, the youngest of four children. At 16 he was playing lead guitar in a rock band, The Kids, with whom he moved to Los Angeles in search of that elusive recording contract. In 1984, his career took a different path when he made his big-screen debut in Wes Craven's A Nightmare on Elm Street. *But it was as Officer Tom Hanson in* 21 Jump Street *that Depp really made his mark, becoming a teen idol in the States, where* US Magazine *voted him one of the ten sexiest bachelors in the entertainment industry. Winona may be gone, and Kate may be on the scene, but the tattoo on his left arm remains 'Winona Forever'.*

Michael Doherty:

In Benny and Joon, Edward Scissorhands, *and* What's Eating Gilbert Grape, *you play offbeat characters who have a maverick, poignant nature. Are you drawn to such roles?*

Johnny Depp:

I guess there's a small line of filament that connects all these characters I play which is, I suppose, the outsider kind of thing. The idea of someone being judged by how they dress or look, the inside being at odds with the outside. They are all sort of Keaton-esque lost souls but I would like to move in a different direction with my career.

MD: *Such as?*

JD: Well, the next film I'm doing is a film called *Ed Wood*. It's about a little-known director.

MD: *He of* Plan 9 From Outer Space *and* Glen or Glenda *fame...*

JD: Yeah that's him! I've always been a fan of his and I'm going to play him in this film. As you know, Ed was a transvestite, but to me that's an interesting part of his personality but secondary to his hunger for making films.

He was desperate to make his films and he would use whatever was around him to complete his projects. I think Ed Wood was talented, man. If you got one of his films and took off the name Edward D. Wood Jr and put on some very elaborate French name, he would be hailed as a fuckin' genius as opposed to one of the worst directors of all time.

MD: *In the early days, you were carving out a career as a rock musician. Would you have been happy if your career had taken you further down that road?*

JD: I don't know if I would have been any happier. You know, it's a strange thing because music was my life for years and in a way it is still my first love. I still play the guitar, it is just that I don't do it for a living any more. Things must happen for one reason or another and for some reason I was pushed into this field.

MD: *What is the most galling thing for you about the whole Hollywood scene?*

JD: The one thing I hate about Hollywood is the judgements that are passed on people. The way they categorise and label you as one particular thing. By that I mean they limit you and it is dangerous for anyone who has sincere drive. For example, I have written a screenplay with my brother which we hope to get produced and I hope to direct.

MD: *You have worked with the likes of John Waters, Tim Burton and Oliver Stone. Which of those diverse directors will have most influence on your own directing style?*

JD: I think it will be a combination. John has always been a great influence on me and a great hero of mine. But the most influential director I ever worked with, simply because we spent so much time together, was a guy named Emir Kusturica who did *Time of the Gypsies* a few years back and then two years ago we did *Arizona Dream* together. I have directed a couple of shorts and the interesting thing about Emir is that he maintains a very strong foundation in his films. He doesn't rely on talking heads or the tight close-up but allows the world to come into the lens. I learnt a lot from Lasse Hallstrom, too, after *What's Eating Gilbert Grape.*

MD: *Has it made you a better actor, knowing what it is like from the opposite side of the camera?*

JD: It has definitely given me perspective. With acting you can go to class, read books, take lessons, but there is no better training than to just do it. And the same applies to directing. Just dive in and try it. But yes, I've been much easier with directors since I started directing, myself!

MD: *I'm interested in what you say about being labelled. Because you appear on the covers of teen magazines, and are always described in terms of a sex symbol, there is a certain amount of baggage that you carry that might jeopardise your chances when a serious role comes along. Do people regard you as the face first and the actor second?*

JD: The labels do bother me but luckily, with the films which I have been able to do, which is based on, I don't know, the air, luck, whatever, I've been able to kill that image which was sort of forced down people's throats. It was an image which had absolutely nothing to do with me.

MD: *Was that a* 21 Jump Street *legacy?*

JD: Well, it started with that and then there were some unimaginative people who needed to sell a product, who labelled me as that product and sold me as that product. But I'm lucky. I've been able to fight them so far. As far as being associated with teenagers, for example, that doesn't bother me at all. They are the future and I find their opinions much more interesting than those of most adults who have become jaded and close-minded.

MD: *How important was Nicolas Cage in your decision to switch from music to acting?*

JD: It's basically all Nic's fault! I owe a lot to him. For some reason he had this feeling that I should attempt acting. It was about ten years ago when he sent me to meet his agent and then, all this happened. Between Nic, my first agent and Wes Craven, who did *Elm Street* and was brave enough to cast somebody who was totally green, I owe those three people a lot.

MD: *Though you have made your name in television and cinema, a lot of journalists seem more interested in your relationship with Winona Ryder...*

JD: The first thing I found amazing was that somebody would be so interested in somebody else's private life: the fascination with what happens between two people when they go home. That to me is pretty amazing because it reaches a certain level when it becomes surreal. I just don't understand that kind of fascination.

MD: *Have you had the attentions of the* National Enquirer *and the rest of them?*

JD: Yes, and the shitty London tabloids and the shitty American tabloids. It doesn't make me angry. It's like a bug flying around. You know it's there and once in a while you swat at it. When I am asked about Winona now, I say, "Oh, we've broken up." It's amazing the reaction that gets from journalists! They stop dead in their tracks and don't know what to ask you next. I get a certain amount of glee from that!

MD: *Would you say* Edward Scissorhands *is your finest hour to date?*

JD: It is a film I relate to and the one with which I am most connected. It was a story that comes around only once in a lifetime. It was also the most difficult one to finish. I remember looking at Edward in the mirror for the last time as I took off the make-up and feeling very depressed! There was some sort of safety in Edward for me, a kind of safety in being that simple and open.

MD: *You don't appear comfortable with fame or celebrity...*

JD: This may sound stupid, but I don't really buy into that celebrity stuff, so I don't think of myself in those terms. I feel like a very, very lucky gas-station attendant. That's what it boils down to for me. It is all down to luck. There are a lot of very unfortunate people in the world and I feel very fortunate that my family is going to be OK if they need anything. To be as successful as someone like Tom Cruise is different. I wouldn't know what to do with that kind of money! Once you reach 20 million, 25 million, 40 million dollars, what the fuck are you going to do with it, man! The only thing I could think to do with it is give it away. How much money does one person need? How much money does Arnie need? Cuban cigars aren't

that expensive!

MD: *Though you don't travel the Hollywood circuit of power lunches and dinner parties, I know you have struck up a close relationship with one of our most popular actors, Gabriel Byrne...*

JD: I have been very down on Hollywood and acting in recent years, but Gabriel is someone I respect deeply and profoundly. He is such a breath of fresh air that he restores your faith in what you do. Most people in Hollywood do things for money, gross points and ambition. Talking to Gabriel and knowing why he does it makes me realise why I do it. I would love to work with Gabriel. As a human being he is absolutely incredible and someone I look up to. And he is one of the finest actors out there. Aidan Quinn is like that, too. He was a revelation. I never met anyone who was so incapable of dishonesty.

MD: *Maybe it's the Irish in them.*

JD: Yeah, it's great here, man. I'm ready to stay here forever, man. I've fallen in love with Ireland. There is such a warmth here and a quality to the people who are so down-to-earth. They don't give a... I guess I can't say it...

MD: *Go on, say it!*

JD: Well, they really don't give a f... about celebrity or status. It makes you feel normal. You don't feel under a glass case. And that feels good.

POSTSCRIPT

Since the interview, Depp has made positive headlines for his performances in Ed Wood *and* Don Juan de Marco *(opposite Marlon Brando), and negative headlines when he was briefly jailed for trashing a hotel room. Other negative reports surrounded the death of his friend, River Phoenix, outside Depp's Sunset Boulevard club, The Viper Room. He has fulfilled one ambition by appearing opposite Gabriel Byrne in the thriller* Deadman. *On a personal level, supermodel Kate Moss remains his constant companion. No sign of a tattoo yet, though.*

MOVIEGUIDE'S 10 LEAST CONVINCING FOREIGN ACCENTS

1   Keanu Reeves's English hero, *Bram Stoker's Dracula* (1993): "Is the kahsal fahh?"

2   Tom Cruise's Irish pugilist, *Far and Away* (1993): "Aye, yer a carker, Shannon" (below).

3 Sean Connery's Soviet submarine commander, *The Hunt For Red October* (1990): "We shail into hishtory."

4 Brooklyn's own Tony Curtis as an, er, Arabian Knight in *The Prince who was a Thief* (1951): "Yonder lies de palace of my fodder, de caliph."

5 Basil Rathbone's French pirate, Captain Lavasseur, in *Captain Blood* (1935): "Vat is ze first order, mon capitan?"

6 Tor Johnson's American cop, *Plan 9 From Outer Space* (1959): "I'm a bik boy now, Johnny."

7 Meryl Streep's Australian, Lyndy Chamberlain, *A Cry in the Dark* (1988): "Dingows got moy bayboy!"

8 Tommy Lee Jones's Irish revolutionary, *Blown Away* (1994): "Bee ido koolah."

9 James Coburn's Aussie POW, *The Great Escape* (1963): "Wat bladdy use is that, moite."

10 Chico Marx's Italian accent in, er, every Marx Brothers film: "Geta your toosie frootsie icea cream."

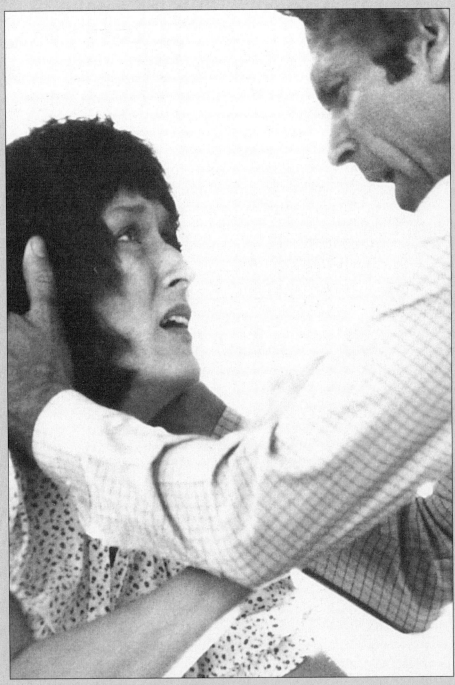

"What is that accent, Meryl?"

TAKE TEN
GEORGE WENDT

The section in which various personalities have been given three minutes to answer ten revealing questions about their cinema-going habits. Next up is George Wendt, better known as Norm in the popular US sitcom, Cheers.

1   *If you were to be stranded on a desert island with nothing but a VCR and three films, what titles would you choose?*

The Godfather and *The Godfather Part II* (Coppola; 1972/74, US); *The Treasure of the Sierra Madre* (Huston; 1948, US); *The Longest Day* (Anakin; 1962, US)

2   *What was the most recent film you saw and how would you rate it out of ten?*

The Secret of Roan Inish. Since I'd like to work in a John Sayles film, I'd give it a ten! Seriously, though, it was a bit too soft for me, too much of a feel-good movie. However, it's difficult to rate movies. That movie was what it was, and it was what it was quite beautifully.

3 *When was the last time you cried at the movies?*

You know, I cry quite frequently at movies but I just can't think of the last time. Of course, I have cried a lot of times on stage.

4 *Who was your first movie star pin-up?*

I honestly can't remember!

5 *What is your attitude to sub-titles?*

I like them. I certainly prefer a sub-titled film to a dubbed film.

6 *How many of the 12 Angry Men can you name?*

I don't think I've ever seen the movie, but from my knowledge of pop culture, I can probably name a few: Ed Begley, Henry Fonda, Lee J. Cobb, Jason Robards?

7 *As a major baseball fan, do you think there has ever been a good baseball movie made?*

I don't think so, but then again, I haven't seen *Field of Dreams*.

8 *Who is the finest actor you have ever seen?*

Al Pacino in his role as Michael Corleone.

9 *If Hollywood were planning to film the story of your life, who would you like to see in the title role?*

Lenny Henry does a good me but I'd like to give someone a real hard stretch. Maybe Jane Fonda or Meryl Streep!

10 *And what would it be called?*

Follow the Shade.

REEL 9

THE MAN
WHO SOLD
THE WORLD

"It's very hip to be all dressed in black: you look like Johnny Cash!"

Tom Hanks is standing in a London hotel room with a broad grin on his face. Although this one is directed at the monochrome journo in front of him, it's not unreasonable to suggest that the actor has had a permanent grin on his face for the past three years. His last four films – Sleepless in Seattle, Philadelphia, Forrest Gump *and now* Apollo 13 *– smashed box-office records, and two of them produced small gold statuettes for the man from Concord, California. In person, Hanks is friendly of demeanour and firm of handshake. Taller than you might think, he happens to be (for a major film star) remarkably ordinary looking. Indeed, if you were a hermit into whose cave he had* *wandered, only the impeccable silk suit would lead you to surmise that this lanky intruder must be a very successful person.*

A few facts about this man in the silk suit. He is 39 years of age; he is married to Rita, his second wife, whom he met on the set of Volunteers; *he received $800 for his first film role (*Forrest Gump *earned him $40 million); he likes space lore (his own film company, Clavius, is named for one of the space stations in* 2001: A Space Odessey, *a film he has seen 30 times); he enjoys surfing in Santa Monica; he is America's Everyman; he uses the word "neat" a lot. Oh yes, and he happens to be the most successful film star on the planet...*

Michael Doherty:

> *You have been described as a 'space junkie'. Is that a fair comment?*

Tom Hanks:

> Well, I'm a space aficionado, and that's a big difference. Actually, I'm a space race scholar! I was well up on the space programme so I came to *Apollo 13* with an awful lot of information in my head. But every step of the way was a continuing education for me. I kept finding out more stuff that was even neater than the stuff I knew.

MD: *What was it like portraying a living, breathing character like Jim Lovell, who you knew would be watching your finished work?*

TH: Very, very intimidating. The first time I met him it was sad. Here I am, this cheesy showbiz personality and I'm actually meeting the guy who did it. We don't look anything alike! We had a

Polaroid taken of us both and when I saw it I said to him, "This looks like Jim Lovell and his pool man!" It was pretty embarrassing.

MD: *This was an extraordinary event which captured the imagination of the world. Why did it take until 1992 to get the book published?*

TH: I think because it was immediately forgotten. It did hold the world's attention for four days but then nobody cared. By that time, 1970, the space program was really over for a lot of people. Neil Armstrong had walked on the moon. End of story. Once they got back safely, also, that story was over. As far as NASA went, the whole episode was swept off to the side because it was a bad thing that happened, a bad mark on their record. NASA suffered huge budget cuts as a result of Apollo XIII. Yet for all the guys who worked on the program, it was a celebratory moment. I was at a reunion of Apollo Mission Control

guys recently and they were saying that the best moments they had were on Apollo VIII, the first time man left Earth's gravity, and Apollo XIII. Apollo XI was fabulous and historical, but they felt best about what they did on Apollo XIII.

MD: *I've heard you mention about the similarities between being an astronaut and being an actor. From your own point of view, you've had a number of moon shots in recent years. How do you explain that phenomenal success?*

TH: I can't explain it other than the movies came out pretty good. That's about the only thing I can say.

MD: But did you read the scripts and go, "This is the Big One"?

TH: I never look at scripts and say, "Hey, this thing is going to do really well." If you are going to look at it that way you are going to be in big, big trouble.

MD: *Is that what happened with* The Bonfire of the Vanities?

TH: That's exactly what happened.

We all said, "Hey, everybody loves this book and hey, this movie should do really well." Insanity. This process is purely an instinctive one for me. I read the story and I think I understand it better than everybody else, I go in loaded with ideas and I usually say, "Will you please let me do this role?" That's the way I've done it of late and it's only sheer luck and the hard work of film-makers I've worked with that has made all this happen. The only decision I made, as far as a philosophy goes on how to choose roles, was to say — I'm not sure if you have the term over here — that I'm not going to play wimps any more! That's the only thing I said.

MD: *When was that?*

TH: That was right about the time I made the baseball movie with Penny Marshall (*A League Of Their Own*). I said to my agents, "I've played the same type of role in the past; ordinary guys who are funny and can't commit to

relationships and they wonder if they are ever going to fall in love again and blah, blah, blah. I'm not doing that any more." That was actually very liberating because it meant that I didn't have to consider 80 per cent of the scripts I was being sent.

MD: *But does this mean you'll stop being America's Everyman, the modern-day James Stewart? Or had you grown tired of that monicker anyway?*

TH: Well, there's nothing I can do to change it. I was tired of it years ago to tell you the truth! But I also understand that I'm a relatively unique presence in Hollywood, because I'm not incredibly good-looking and I'm not a striking physical presence.

MD: *Yet in the Hollywood* Vanity Fair *you were described as one of The Three Kings, alongside the striking physical presence that is Arnold Schwarzenegger and the incredibly good-looking presence that is Tom Cruise...*

TH: Yeah, that's right; how did I get in there! That's just the current vogue. If you look at anyone who's in the top five for any year in the history of Hollywood, there's always a couple of people who lead you to say, "What's that guy doing in there?" John Wayne, Gary Cooper, Van Johnson ... Van Johnson? That might be where I am, as a matter of fact, and that's OK. I don't threaten anybody when I come on screen. Nobody fears me, I'm not a huge mystery to anybody when I walk out there. In some ways, because I have been doing it for so long, I might be a reassuring presence. So the job for me becomes to surprise those people somehow, and as long as I have the access to the material to surprise those people, then I should be slightly ahead of the curve.

MD: *Now that you are ahead of the curve, what do you do to relax?*

TH: Well, I go to films and try to see everything. But there are three very specific modes. When I am actually working on a movie, it is all-encompassing and every day. When you are promoting a movie you are gone for weeks at a time. But when I am not working, I have an office I go to for a couple of hours a week and the rest of the time I'm watering the lawn and taking the kids to the dentist and all that stuff.

MD: *And can Tom Hanks do all that stuff without being besieged?*

TH: In Los Angeles or New York I can but not any other place. But I live in Los Angeles and it's a standard kind of industry town.

MD: *But the fame hasn't become a burden?*

TH: Sometimes it is a burden because we live in very complex times. I've been lucky because my celebrity has grown incrementally in the course of ten years. You learn how to deal with that and you learn how to be protected. There are things you learn how to do for not only my security, but for the security of my wife, Rita and my kids. But it's not hard to do it in a sane way. It's easy to become like Elvis in the compound and never go anywhere. Hollywood is littered with the corpses of people who live that way because they went stark, raving nuts!

MD: *Two Oscars, the biggest movie of all time and a salary of $15 million per film... Any unfulfilled ambitions?*

TH: Well, I'm not a real ambitious guy, to tell you the truth. I never sat down and said, "By such and such an age I would like to have experienced this." The most important thing I have done in the last ten years, besides have kids of course, was to learn how to surf. I never thought I could learn it and I'm a pretty decent surfer now. Once I had got that whipped, I felt that I had pretty much accomplished everything!

MD: *So when's the surfing movie coming out?*

TH: Man, as soon as we can figure out a way of making it happen! Wouldn't that be great? Have you ever seen *Endless Summer*, Michael? What a great gig that was.

MD: Endless Summer *was good, but what about* Big Wednesday*?*

TH: You know what, I think you would be hard pressed to make a better movie than *Big Wednesday*. That movie made me cry. There's a scene in that where the muscular guy goes over to William Katt who is heading off to Vietnam and just says, "Come back to us." That kills me every time! Great stuff. Surf movie: that's got to be my next move.

IN LIKE FLYNN

Errol Flynn

Though his reputation has been dominated by off-screen scandals and an early death (at 50) which owed much to his picaresque lifestyle of booze (he shared a house with David Niven called Cirrhosis-by-the-Sea), drugs and women, Errol Flynn was a true cinema original. Never a brilliant actor, he was, nonetheless, one of the screen's great heroic figures who put swashbucklers such as Douglas Fairbanks and Tyrone Power in the shade.

Born in Hobart, Tasmania, Flynn played up his Irish heritage when he arrived in Hollywood and Warner Brothers were quick to respond to his roguish charm. *Captain Blood* (1935) first saw him in swashbuckling mode, but it was *The Adventures of Robin Hood* (1938) which made him a star. As the legendary English hero, Flynn displayed all the athletic

swagger ("Are you with me, men?") and braggadoccio that would inform his best performances. In truth, Flynn only made a handful of what could be called classic films, the last being *Rocky Mountain* in 1950, but his bravura screen persona was such that he remains one of the Hollywood greats. "I allow myself to be understood as a colour fragment in a drab world," he wrote in his memoirs, *My Wicked, Wicked Ways* (ghosted by Earl Conrad), and the screen would certainly have been more drab without the presence of Errol Flynn.

THE PICK OF FLYNN

The Adventures of Robin Hood (1938)
"It's injustice I hate, not Normandy!" Flynn swashbuckles his way into the heart of Olivia De Havilland and firmly establishes himself as the dashing, heroic figure of his generation. Curtiz's dazzling film is filled with romance, action and Korngold's superb score; and all in glorious technicolor. Beware recent cheap imitations: Errol Flynn is the one true Robin Hood, a man who speaks treason fluently and can look dashing even while wearing lime green tights.

They Died with Their Boots On (1941)
Anybody who knows anything about General George Custer realises that this biopic is sheer hokum, but no matter. Director Raoul Walsh shows an instinctive flair for presenting Flynn and he gets a bravura performance from his actor. This was the eighth and final teaming of Flynn and De Havilland, and the chemistry is still there in force. The scene in which Flynn leaves his wife knowing he will never return is supremely touching.

Gentleman Jim (1942)
The best of the Walsh/Flynn collaborations offered the actor a tailor-made role: the charming and cocky Irish-American champion boxer, Jim Corbett, a man equally adept with word and fist. The sparks between Flynn and Alexis Smith are not of De Havilland proportions but it's obvious that Flynn is relishing the role.

BRAVE AT HEART

"God, I hate this stuff!"

Mel Gibson is quite a sight. One of the most famous actors in the world is standing in a cow pat-strewn field in Ballymore Eustace, covered in dirt, grass and the substance which bears the brunt of his grievance, sticky fake blood. From his shoulder protrudes the remnants of an English arrow. His face is a mass of sweat, blood and war paint, overhung by a tangled fright wig, which itself bears all the hallmarks of recent skirmishes. No amount of talcum powder proffered by the assistant can ease the actor's obvious discomfort. Anyone who believes that film-making is a glamorous profession would do well to cop a gander at Mr Gibson.

The actor is here shooting *Braveheart*, the true story of the struggle between Scottish hero, Sir William Wallace, and the English king, Edward the First, known as the Hammer of the Scots, during the Scottish Wars of Independence at the turn of the fourteenth century. The scene being shot is the pivotal confrontation between Wallace and Robert Bruce at the Battle of Falkirk, where a heavily outnumbered Scots force was massacred by Edward and his archers in 1298.

Take after take, Mel swings into action, demonstrating why he is considered one of the most physical of today's actors. One particular set-up is delayed by the sun making a feeble attempt to appear. Meanwhile it has begun to drizzle. "I can't check the sun reading," bemoans the director of photography, "because the rain is falling on my lens!" Welcome to Ireland, folks.

Between shots, Mel the star becomes Mel the director as he retires to a makeshift lean-to where he can survey the rushes. "Come here and I'll show you this," he beckons, bringing my attention to footage of a battle scene which employs the use of mechanical horses for the close-up shots. "No trip-wires and no animal gets hurt. Except for the odd beetle of course. In fact, I was talking to a beetle the

other day," Mel continues, as the assembled crew grin knowingly, "and I said to him, 'Do you realise that there was a very famous group named after you?' 'What,' says the beetle, 'there's a group called Dennis?'"

Not the best joke in the world, granted, but symptomatic of the rapport which Gibson has with the cast and crew. The laughter is not forced and the groans are genuine. Mel may be star, director and producer, but he is still one of the lads. No extra-long trailer and no tantrums. He shares everything with those around him; his opinions, his jokes and his lunch break.

Over on the far side of the field, members of the FCA are crashed out, another exhausting battle clocked up. Splendidly attired in their shields, mail gloves and padded tunics, many bear plastic re-presentations of the famous 12-foot spears which the Scots expertly deployed in formations known as schiltrons. Others look so frightening that it is a wonder that they needed weapons at all (Brendan Gleeson, for example, makes Atilla the Hun look like Deanna Durbin).

Back on the main set, take

number three has taken its toll on Mel, and he lets out a howl as he spins to the ground. An earlier leg wound, for which he has been employing the use of a local chiropractor, has resurfaced and it's clear that the man is in some pain. To add insult to his injury, the rain has begun to fall again. "Lunch!" cries the assistant director, and all hands dutifully repair to the marquees.

Lunch proves quite an experience as an assortment of battered, blooded and bruised extras queue for their meat and two veg. As I take my seat in a quiet spot, Mel ambles over in a blue towelling dressing gown, making light of his recent injury and dismissive of the suggestion that he might now be regretting appearing on both sides of the camera for such a physical project. "At this stage," he concedes, "I would be more inclined to say, 'I wish I had gotten another actor to do it.' But it's too late."

So, the $64,000 question, why make a film about William Wallace? "He was committed and he was unbreakable," says Mel, with some conviction. "People like him come up from time to time in history.

They don't live long, they never do. They have a penchant for telling the truth and putting people's noses out of joint. Wallace is a dreamer who wants something better. He figures he has a right to something better; like freedom. Personally, I think that he was pretty fierce in battle, that was his deal. I don't know where that came from, whether he didn't give a shit, or what. He just wanted to put it all on the line. It's like the character says in the film, 'I'd rather be dead than enslaved'."

So profit wasn't a motive, as was the case with many of the feudal lords at the time? "There doesn't seem to be any evidence that he was doing it for profit," says Mel. "I looked for those motives, I really did. He was offered things but he didn't take them. On a purist level, he was only concerned with his freedom and his country. Most people who profess to share that view are more concerned with lining their pockets. He was one of the exceptions."

Making *Braveheart* for his own company, Icon Productions (which has just finished shooting *Immortal Beloved* in Prague), means that Gibson has more than a vested

Reel Lives

interest in the success or failure of the film. Despite this, he is not worried that mainstream US audiences might be inclined to go 'William Who?' or balk at the idea of shelling out their hard-earned lucre for a film which concerns itself with fourteenth-century Scottish history.

"I have no worries on that score," says Mel, confidently. The story is very strong and the characters are very strong. It has the whole gamut in there, from a political thriller to a great love story to great action. Commercially, you look at these things, you have to."

Braveheart is the second film which has taken Mel behind the camera. The first, *The Man Without a Face*, proved that the actor could handle helming duties and didn't waste all those years looking up the lens at the likes of George Miller and Richard Donner. As a result, he is firmly installed as one of Hollywood's power players but still, famously, finds plenty of time for his wife, Robyn, and their six children.

"You just find the time to do it, somehow," says Mel. "There's a balance in there and sometimes you reach it and sometimes you don't but you will get it back eventually. In

a wider picture you will always get the balance."

As, still covered in fake blood, paint and straggles of the fright wig covering his face, he wolfs down the pork chop and spuds, it is only the piercing blue eyes that remind one that Mel Gibson has been carrying that sex symbol tag for much of his career. It is not a label he wears willingly, not surprisingly, given the presence of films such as *Tim*, *Gallipoli*, *The Year of Living Dangerously* and, the film which really opened many people's eyes to Mel's thespian abilities, *Hamlet*. "I'm not too concerned about those labels," says Mel, dismissively. "It doesn't make any difference, really. I'm getting by. People give me money to do this, so I'm happy."

By the same token, the 38-year-old actor has never been over-enamoured with the degree of fame that success in the film business has brought him. "You don't enjoy that level of fame, or at least it's not something I enjoy. I think Joan Collins enjoys it and that's fine. If she digs it, great. There are upsides and downsides and it all kind of evens out. I don't go out, anywhere. Not because I don't want to go out.

I can't. I can't go anywhere. You spend every minute in a popular situation giving all your energy to everyone else; and that's just a pain in the ass. I'm just drained at the end of it. I would just like to go somewhere quiet but I haven't found the place yet."

So is there nowhere on the globe that people don't recognise Mel Gibson?

"Sure, the Simpson Desert!"

Fame, indeed, seems a genuine burden to the New York-born, Australian-reared actor. But the man whose films have garnered over $1 billion in box-office receipts, and who has been known to give women the world over a touch of the vapours, is aware of the stresses that come with the job. "I'm an easy man to work with, most of the time," he concedes. "But I've lost it a few times because it can get stressful. If something is not there I get crazy. But I wouldn't have got so cranky

five years ago. Believe me, my patience with it is a lot shorter than it used to be. Funny, isn't it? I don't know whether it is wisdom or boredom."

For the former altar boy who recalls being a "falter boy" wont to set fire to his garments by day-dreaming near the candles, the punishing schedule is, at times, "ridiculous", but Mel Gibson continues to be driven by the need to tell a good story, aided by a wicked sense of humour, which provides the perfect release mechanism. "If you can't get out of it any other way," concludes Mel, "just make 'em laugh. You have to have that."

And a little faith?

"You have to have faith," says Mel, polishing off the last spud. "You must have these things. Otherwise, what the f... am I doing? What the f... is anyone doing?"

REEL LIVES' QUIZ COMPETITION - Exciting Prizes to be won

This section of the book introduces the Reel Lives' Quiz, which will test your film knowledge and spark off some interesting debates between family members! When you have answered the questions from the various sections, just jot them down and send them in to the Reel Lives' Quiz competition, Blackwater Press, Unit 8, Broomhill Business Park, Tallaght, Dublin 24. Please enclose the competition entry form with your entry. The closing date for the competition is February 1, 1996. All prizes will be drawn on 5 February 1996. Winners will be notified by post, and will be listed in the *RTE Guide*.

First Prize
The first name out of the hat with all the correct answers will win a fabulous long weekend for two at the Champagne Bollinger vineyards, courtesy of Bollinger and UIP. Situated in Ay in the heart of France's Champagne region, Bollinger is style, and is both a champagne house and an institution. Its extraordinary quality is anchored in a great family tradition and is legendary among wine lovers. Little wonder that Pierce Brosnan's James Bond will accept nothing less in the latest 007 film, *Goldeneye*.

The lucky winners will fly directly from Dublin to Paris with Aer Lingus and then transfer to the famed family château, to be wined and dined for three nights. The weekend will include tours of the vineyards and cellars in the company of Guy Bizot, a key member in the Bollinger family, affording a chance to enjoy some of the wonderful French countryside.

Second Prize
The second name out of the hat will receive this cool *Apollo 13* jacket, worth £250, which may or may not have been worn by Tom Hanks in the Ron Howard movie.

Third Prize
The third prizewinner will receive a selection of merchandising goodies from Buena Vista's smash Christmas film, *The Santa Clause*, starring Tim Allen.

Fourth Prize
Fourth prize is a copy of the first draft script from *Reservoir Dogs*, signed by the most acclaimed writer/director of our time, Quentin Tarantino.

Fifth Prize
The fifth prizewinner will receive a Director's Chair. Now you can pretend to be a Hollywood big-shot in the comfort of your own bedroom.
In addition, we have fifteen videos, comprising titles from Tarantino, Brando, Lancaster and a selection of war films, which will be handed out to winners six through twenty, as they are pulled from the Reel Lives' hat.

Good luck!

REEL LIVES' COMEDY QUIZ

1   Which US television series first brought Jim Carrey to public attention?

2   "A strange man defecated on my sister." A line from which Woody Allen film?

3   Which Oscar-winning actress provided the voice of the brain in *The Man with Two Brains*, starring Steve Martin?

4   Which seventies screwball comedy revolved around a plaid overnight bag and starred an actress who had won an Oscar, Emmy and Grammy?

5   "You're awfully shy for a lawyer."
"I know, I'm a shyster lawyer."
Clearly Groucho. But the film?

6   Which musical instrument did Jack Lemmon's character (male and female) play in *Some Like it Hot*?

7   What was the name of Nick and Norah's dog in the *Thin Man* series?

8   "I'll have what she's having!" The film?

9   In which film does Gene Wilder go to bed with an Armenian sheep named Daisy?

10   What comes next in the following sequence: Sergeant, Nurse, Teacher, Constable, ...?

REEL LIVES' MUSIC QUIZ

1   Russ Tamblyn led The Jets, but who was the leader of The Sharks?

2   With which Italian/American tenor were the Heavenly Creatures infatuated?

3   Two football anthems, "Que Sera Sera" and "You'll Never Walk Alone" featured in films released in 1956. Name them.

4   His first film score was *Citizen Kane*, his last was *Taxi Driver*. Who was he?

5   "I Love You Samantha", "Now You Has Jazz", "Who Wants to be a Millionaire"... The musical?

6   To which song did John and Uma perform the twist in Tarantino's *Pulp Fiction*?

7   Complete the pairings from a famous Forties musical: Frank Sinatra and Betty Garrett, Gene Kelly and Vera-Ellen, Jules Munshin and ...?

8   When Fred Astaire famously danced on the walls and ceiling of his hotel room, the song was 'You're All the World to Me'. But what was the film?

9   Marni Nixon dubbed the likes of Natalie Wood and Audrey Hepburn on screen, but in which film, one of the all-time highest grossers, did we both see and hear Ms Nixon?

10   "Moses supposes his toses are roses..." The film?

REEL LIVES' QUOTATIONS QUIZ

The following quotations are all taken from famous films. Identify the films in question and the actors responsible for each remark or exchange.

1   "If you had come to me in friendship then this scum that ruined your daughter would be suffering this very day. And if by chance an honest man like yourself should make enemies, then they would become my enemies. And then they would fear you."

2   "Tell me, who runs up that flag — your wife?"
"No, my flag steward."
"And who mixes the cocktails — your wife?"
"No, my cocktail steward. Look, if you're interested in whether I'm married or not — "
"I'm not interested at all."
"Well, I'm not."
"That's very interesting."

3   "Don't get sore at me. I'm not an executive. I'm just a writer."
"You are! Writing words, words! You've made a rope of words and strangled this business! But there is a microphone right there to capture the last gurgles, and Technicolor to photograph the red, swollen tongue!"
"Shh. You'll wake up that monkey."

4   "Nature, Mr Allnut, is what we're put into this world to rise above."

5   "You gonna bark all day, little doggie, or are you gonna bite?"
"What was that? I'm sorry, I didn't catch it."
"I said: 'Are you gonna bark all day, doggie, or are you gonna bite?'"

6   "Not that I care, but where is your husband?"
"Why, he's dead."
"I'll bet he's just using that as an excuse."
"I was with him to the very end."
"No wonder he passed away."
"I held him in my arms and kissed him."
"Oh, I see, then it was murder. Will you marry me? Did he leave you any money? Answer the second question first."

7   "Fasten your seat-belts. It's going to be a bumpy night."

8   "Well, I know how you feel about me, but I'm asking you to put your feelings aside for something more important."
"Do I have to hear again what a great man your husband is? What an important cause he's fighting for?"
"It was your cause, too. In your own way, you were fighting for the same thing."
"I'm not fighting for anything any more, except myself. I'm the only cause I'm interested in."

9   "There'll be no locks and bolts between us, Mary Kate, except those in your own mercenary little heart."

10   "Today, war is too important to be left to the politicians. They have neither the time, the training or the inclination for strategic thought. I can no longer sit back and allow Communist infiltration, Communist subversion and the international Communist conspiracy to sap and impurify all of our precious bodily fluids."

REEL LIVES' TOUGH GUYS AND GALS QUIZ

1   In what film did sniggering Tommy Udo (Richard Widmark) push an old lady in a wheelchair down a flight of stairs?

2   "If you say three, mister, you'll never hear the man count ten." Strong words spoken in an Irish bar by erstwhile Trooper Thorn. The film?

3   "You're not very intelligent: I like that in a man." Forties dialogue; Eighties film — the actress?

4   In Luc Besson's *Leon*, which is the only one of Nathalie Portman's impersonations that Jean Reno recognises?

5   "If I'd been a ranch, they'd have named me the Bar Nothing." The gal in question?

6   "If you want to call me that, smile." The Gary Cooper film?

7   Clint was the Good and Lee was Bad; who played the Ugly?

8   Which of The Magnificent Seven was particularly handy with a knife?

9   Which actor took part in *The Gunfight at the OK Corral* (1957) before later going on to battle Klingons?

10   In which country did Butch and Sundance make their final stand?

REEL LIVES' FINAL REEL QUIZ

1   In which film did OJ Simpson hand a cat to Fred Astaire?

2   What Frankenstein was a real Pratt?

3   Who appeared in both *The Godfather* and *The Godfather: Part III*, but changed gender between films?

4   Name three Hitchcock films that begin with the letter S? (*Psycho* not allowed!)

5   Which playing card triggered off Laurence Harvey in *The Manchurian Candidate*?

6   Which of The Great Escapers panicked in the tunnel before making off in a boat?

7   Why was it useful that Fred MacMurray's apartment door opened outwards in *Double Indemnity*?

8   Which poet came into vogue following the release of *Four Weddings and a Funeral*?

9   Only one of the following actors was born in America. Which one? — Keanu Reeves, Mel Gibson, Cary Grant.

10 How many of the actors interviewed in *Reel Lives* have won Oscars?

COMPETITION ENTRY FORM

Name: _____

Address: _____

_____

_____

Telephone: _____

Please attach the answers to the quizzes to this form and post to Movieguide Quiz Competition, Blackwater Press, Unit 8, Broomhill Business Park, Tallaght, Dublin 24.

Competition Rules

1. Entries must be submitted no later than 1 February 1996.
2. Please ensure that this competition entry form is included with each entry. Photocopies will not be accepted.
3. The decision of the judging panel is final, no appeals will be considered.
4. Employees of Blackwater Press and their families are prohibited from submitting entries.
5. All entries to be sent to: Movieguide Quiz Competition, Blackwater Press, c/o Folens Publishers, Unit 8, Broomhill Business Park, Broomhill Road, Tallaght, Dublin 24.
6. All winners will be notified by post, and will be listed in the *RTE Guide*.

BLACKWATER PRESS